The Undersea Discoveries of Jacques-Yves Cousteau

DIVING COMPANIONS
Sea Lion, Elephant Seal, Walrus

In the same series

THE SHARK: Splendid Savage of the Sea
(by Jacques-Yves Cousteau and Philippe Cousteau)

LIFE AND DEATH IN A CORAL SEA
(by Jacques-Yves Cousteau with Philippe Diolé)

DIVING FOR SUNKEN TREASURE
(by Jacques-Yves Cousteau and Philippe Diolé)

THE WHALE: Mighty Monarch of the Sea
(by Jacques-Yves Cousteau and Philippe Diolé)

OCTOPUS AND SQUID: The Soft Intelligence
(by Jacques-Yves Cousteau and Philippe Diolé)

THREE ADVENTURES: Galápagos, Titicaca, The Blue Holes
(by Jacques-Yves Cousteau and Philippe Diolé)

The Undersea Discoveries
of Jacques-Yves Cousteau

DIVING COMPANIONS
Sea Lion, Elephant Seal, Walrus

Jacques-Yves Cousteau
and Philippe Diolé

Translated from the French by J. F. Bernard

Doubleday & Company, Inc.
Garden City, New York 1974

Library of Congress Cataloging in Publication Data

Cousteau, Jacques Yves.
  Diving companions.

  (The Undersea discoveries of Jacques-Yves Cousteau)
  Translation of Compagnons de plongée.
  Bibliography: p.
  1. Sea lions. 2. Elephant seals. 3. Walruses.
I. Diolé, Philippe, joint author. II. Title.
QL737.P6C6813   599'.745
ISBN 0-385-00031-6
Library of Congress Catalog Card Number 73-20508

CONTENTS

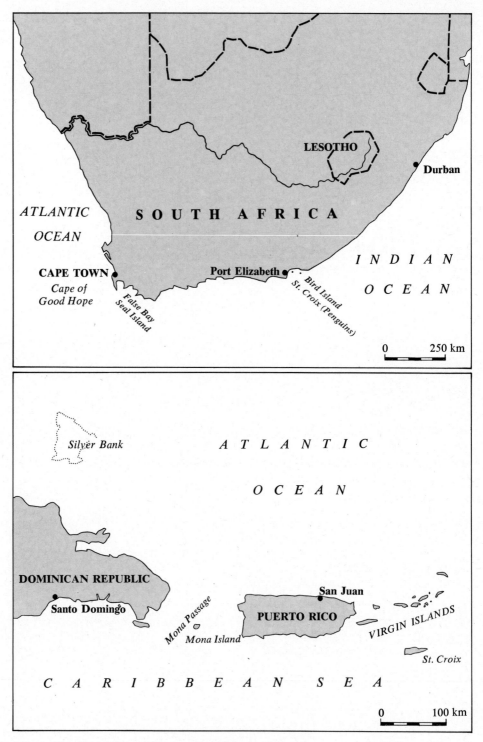

Above: The Cape of Good Hope and neighboring islands
Below: The Caribbean isles, Puerto Rico, and the Virgin Islands

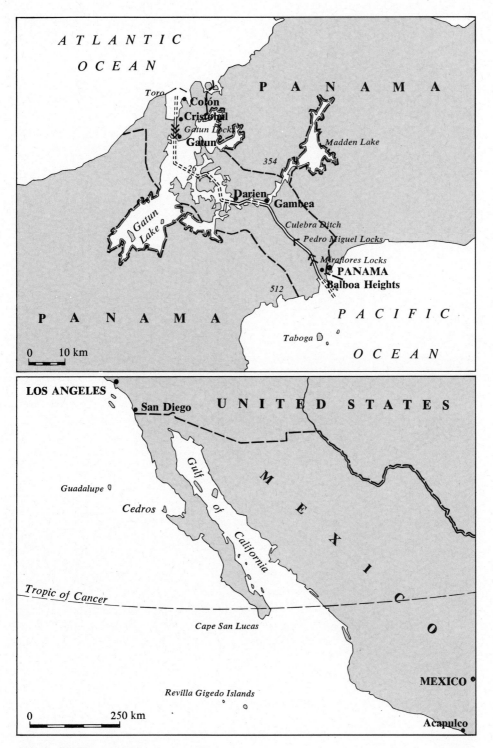

Above: The Panama Canal
Below: The Pacific coast of Mexico

PART ONE
Sea Lion

One

Gannets, Penguins, and Sea Lions

At the end of the winter of 1967, *Calypso* was in the southern region of the Indian Ocean after a long cruise which had led from Aden to the Maldive Islands. It was nearly a year since we had left Monaco and for almost the whole time we were plagued with bad weather. Twice we had had serious mechanical problems. The first time, our starboard propeller broke while we were shooting a film on sperm whales, and we were compelled to cross the whole of the Indian Ocean on one engine, at five knots. The second time, the same propeller broke again — this time in the middle of a hurricane off Europa Island.

We were scheduled to begin a new phase of our forty-two-month expedition after rounding the Cape of Good Hope. We intended to set a course across the Atlantic, toward the Caribbean, where a difficult assignment in marine archaeology awaited us. Then, we would continue on into the Pacific and head toward the Far North.

Aboard *Calypso*, Philippe Cousteau helps his father suit up for a dive

At least, so we thought. The Indian Ocean was not through with us yet. Between Port Elizabeth and the Cape, at the southernmost point of Africa, we decided to send several of our teams to explore a group of little-known islands, which are nothing more than uninhabited rocks in the sea, in the hope that we might be able to film animals which had not yet learned to flee from man. The islands which seemed to offer the best opportunity were in the archipelago off Port Elizabeth: the Black Rocks. We had been there on several occasions, and we had always been able to get some worth-while footage.

The Home of the Boobies

One of the Black Rocks is called Bird Island. We landed there first, hoping to be able to film some seals. But the Union of South Africa knows how to protect her animals. Our three launches set out for shore carrying our diving equipment, cameras, lights, and other necessary supplies. Before they reached land, they were almost overturned by the enormous swell and by a treacherous sandbar. But that was only the beginning of our trouble. When we finally stepped ashore on what we assumed was a deserted rock, we found a man waiting for us. He introduced himself as the lighthouse keeper and asked to see our written authorization to land on Bird Island. When we admitted that we had no such papers, he told us that under no circumstance could we remain on the island. Then, when we apologized and promised to apply immediately for the papers at Port Elizabeth, he relented somewhat and allowed us to look around a bit.

What astonished us was the number of marine birds. There was an incredible crowd of black and white gannets — or boobies as they are called in the United States. They are imposing birds, with green beaks and yellow heads.

The island is only three or four hundred yards wide. With such a large bird population, it is not difficult to believe that it was quite literally covered with guano (sea-bird manure), which is gathered three times yearly and sold commercially. The annual collections net a total of about 100 tons of guano.

There are so many gannets on Bird Island that they form a compact, squalling mass. In order to walk, one has to push them aside with one's feet. The din, as one can imagine, is deafening. We discovered, to our astonishment, that no matter how crowded for space the birds may be, they always manage to leave an empty strip of land in their midst: a take-off strip, which the gannets wait patiently to use in turn.

Gannets feed on fish, and the water between Bird Island and *Calypso* was thick with birds diving from six to ten feet below the surface. Since the water is rich in life, they almost invariably came up with a struggling, splashing fish. When a gannet catches a fish, he immediately returns to Bird Island, to the nest where the female is watching for him. When she sees her mate, she uses her beak against the birds around her to make a place for him. The male lands, like a rock, and the female takes the fish.

We returned to *Calypso* in time to receive a weather report, which was as discouraging as usual. We weighed anchor at 4 P.M. and got underway in a heavy sea, in a forty-knot wind. We had already decided to take shelter at Port Elizabeth.

Saint Croix Island

Sunday, February 25. Jean-Michel Cousteau, my older son, who was the man in South Africa in charge of our supplies and of the logistics of our expedition, was notified by radio of our arrival. He came aboard with good news; by tomorrow, we will have the papers that are apparently necessary for us to be able to work on the Black Rocks.

Meanwhile, at the suggestion of some local divers, we decided to send a team to visit Saint Croix Island. Falco and Bonnici went ahead, to see whether the island was worth a visit from *Calypso*. Our South African friends picked up the two men on the beach, in a Land Rover. Behind the vehicle, there was a skiff on a trailer, carrying two 18 hp outboards. They drove until they were about thirty miles from Capetown, and came to a stop on a beach. The waves were rather high and broke on the sand with a noise like thunder; but the divers, without a moment's hesitation, launched their little boat and set out at full speed in the midst of the waves, with our men holding on for their lives to anything that was secure in the skiff. It is just as well that they did. When the boat reached the bar, it was lifted completely out of the water and tossed a distance of six feet. Everyone was thrown about. The man — a giant — sitting next to Bonnici, landed squarely on him and almost broke his arm. South Africans are an athletic, fun-loving people, and our friends greatly enjoyed "scaring the Frenchmen" a bit; but it was all in fun and was accepted in the same spirit.

It took half an hour to reach Saint Croix Island. The little boat darted through the breakers — some of them fifteen feet high — and was moored in shallow water. Then, the rest of the distance was covered by swimming.

The South Africans were right about Saint Croix. It is inhabited by antarctic penguins, and these animals have taken the island as their own. Neither

Bird Island, off Port Elizabeth, is home to an enormous population of black-and-white boobies

Falco nor Bonnici had ever seen so many of the birds. There were some even at the highest point of the island, at about one hundred feet, where they rubbed shoulders with sea gulls and black cormorants, whose red beaks stood out like bright flowers.

Falco and Bonnici were fascinated. Penguins are strange birds, unable to fly. It is not known for certain whether or not, at some time in their history, they were able to do so. The ancestors of penguins were flying birds, and the penguins' flippers are the remains of their wings. The fossil remains of a giant antarctic penguin, which was about the size of a man and must have weighed well over two hundred pounds, have been found. In any case, penguins are

Saint Croix has been colonized by penguins

obviously quite at home in the water, and they are able to attain speeds of between fifteen and twenty miles per hour.

Falco regretfully concluded that the water was too rough around the island for us to be able to film these birds in the sea. The men therefore amused themselves by watching the penguins marching one behind the other, like soldiers on parade, in perfect step. When the men attempted to draw nearer, however, the penguins ran to the edge of a rock and slid down, occasionally catching themselves to slow their descent, until they splashed into the water. Only the penguins that were setting did not flee. They stood with their single egg between their feet and hidden by their stomachs. The reason for their bravery was obvious. If they had left their eggs, the latter would have immediately been exposed to the gannets and the gulls, which would have carried them away in their beaks.

At 5:30 P.M., everyone swam out to the skiff, and the trip back, at full speed through the breakers, was an exercise in audacity. The giant South African, who had jokingly attempted to crush Bonnici on the trip out to the island, was even more daring than his friends; he swam to shore.

Games of the Penguins

Falco and Bonnici's enthusiastic reports convinced us that a visit to Saint Croix was worth *Calypso*'s while. The following day, February 26, we raised anchor and reached the island in an hour and a quarter. Our launches were lowered into the water, and they crossed the bar less spectacularly than the South Africans had, but with less danger to men and material.

Pierre Goupil was in charge of the exterior shots; and Michel Deloire dived with his movie camera but was unable to get any footage. Falco had been right. The water was so cloudy that it was impossible to shoot. We therefore filmed the penguins on land, from every conceivable angle. Our favorite subjects were the baby penguins, who are so serious and so clumsy as to be extremely comical.

Falco suddenly had an extraordinary idea. There was a shallow natural lake in the middle of the island, he explained, where the water was relatively clear. If he herded the penguins – gently – toward the lake, Deloire could be in the water, with his camera at the ready, and get all the shots he wanted. Like most of Falco's ideas, it worked, and Deloire got some unusual footage.

Calypso remained at anchor overnight, and the next day was given over entirely to filming the penguins. On this occasion, our team was composed of Bernard Chauvelin, Dr. Millet, Pierre Goupil, and Michel Deloire. When the men reached shore, they found the penguins grouped in the middle of the rocks, in clusters of twenty-five or thirty individuals.

Michel Deloire now concluded that the creatures were more afraid of humans than of the boobies. When they are frightened, they scream, but their screams are not strident. Then they flee, moving clumsily. Seen from behind, when they are running away, the penguins look as though they are wearing jackets thrown over their shoulders, and the jackets are swaying from side to side. Despite their apparent clumsiness, they move over the uneven ground with surprising speed, and with greater ease than our men were able to do, because their webbed feet are quite supple and conform to the irregularities of the rocks. Sometimes they seem to be seized with a sudden panic and slide down into the water on their backsides or their stomachs; or they simply throw themselves into the water from heights of as much as six feet.

Bernard Chauvelin discovered a whole group of females which seemed to have gathered to sit on their eggs together. They did not try to run away as he approached, so he was able to inspect them closely. Like many birds, penguins cannot see face-front. The females watched Chauvelin, leaning sometimes to the right and sometimes to the left, staring at him successively with their round, black eyes and conveying an unmistakable impression of astonished indignation.

Meanwhile, on one of the coasts of the island, the other penguins were playing a highly organized game, sliding down a slope on their backsides into the water like children on a slide. As soon as they were in the water, they climbed out and started for the top of the slope so as to begin all over again.

Late in the afternoon, for some mysterious reason, the penguins split into groups of about ten individuals and headed toward the highest point of the island, for all the world like nuns on pilgrimage. On their short journey, they followed the well-defined paths which they have beaten across the island. Each of these paths seems to correspond to one of the activities to which they devote various parts of the day.

When the penguins reached their destination, the cormorants were sitting on their nests, and there was a great hue and cry. The birds exchanged a few blows with their beaks, most of which were off target, and there were a few wing blows, equally wide of the mark. Despite their greater size, the penguins seemed to get the worst of the skirmish. Finally, they retreated with great dignity, in single file, while the cormorants, which a moment before had

Following page: Young sea lions take their first swimming lessons in a pool in the interior of their island

Two boobies confront one another in a ritual display

been shrieking and flapping, settled back calmly onto their nests.

What was the meaning of this little drama? Is it a token exercise of ownership on the part of the penguins? That is, an act designed to vindicate their proprietorship over the entire island, including the summit, but without committing themselves to all-out war? It is impossible to know, of course. But it is interesting to note that this little ceremony takes place regularly, once a day, in the evening.

Our team captured, ever so gently, a penguin in order to examine it. The bird was so unhappy at his detention that they released it almost immediately. In the few minutes during which they were able to observe it, however, they noted that there is a thin, movable membrane over the eye, which obviously affects its sight. The penguin, as soon as it was released, shook itself and walked away, chattering in outrage, the very picture of an elegant gentleman whose dignity has been injured.

A Skeleton

Despite the threatening weather and an increasingly rough sea, a team led by Bébert Falco went on to explore a small island near Bird Island. They found the island overrun with black rabbits, darting about in high, thick grass. They also saw penguins in the grass, which is unusual, for penguins are ordinarily partial to rocky sites.

What kind of rabbits are these, and where do they come from? A miniature mystery.

In the middle of the island, Bébert's team came across the skeleton of an immense whale. It seemed whole, with its vertebrae, huge ribs, and round skull all intact. It must have taken a storm of unusual force to have deposited the whale there. The island is low and flat, but the skeleton was found fifteen to twenty feet above sea level.

There were also a great number of birds constantly taking off and landing, mostly gannets whose screeches rose and fell like the shouts of an angry mob. Despite this unflattering simile, the gannet is by no means an unattractive animal. It has a well-formed head covered by soft, reddish-brown plumage. Its beak is long and blue. Its eyes are circled in blue, and its long, graceful neck is backed with lovely light-blue feathers. The body is white; the wings and tail feathers, black. The feet are webbed, with a network of greenish tracings over the toes. Goupil filmed the birds, while Marcelin taped their cries.

The team reached *Calypso* with great difficulty. The weather had taken a turn for the worse, and we decided to find shelter at Port Elizabeth.

February 28. En route from Port Elizabeth to Capetown. Foul weather and a heavy swell.

The Sea Lions

February 29. Calypso is anchored off Geyser Island.

Falco took a team ashore and immediately telephoned *Calypso,* suggesting that we move in as close as possible to shore. He also suggested that we

Following page: The sea lions swimming off the Cape of Good Hope. At this point, our divers had not yet been able to get near them in the open water

send in all our film equipment. It seems that there are about a hundred sea lions on Geyser Island.

The water is rather clear, and the bottom has a good growth of kelp, very similar to that we saw in California.

We were struck immediately by the extraordinary stench emanating from the island. The young sea lions were bathing on shore, learning to swim in the midst of excrement and urine.

Dr. Millet discovered a small sea lion with a hook in its eye. He succeeded in removing it, but, since he had no medication with him, that was all he could do. He says that the animal will probably be blind permanently in that eye.

We took our shark cages with us, since one never knows what will be the reaction of such animals as sea lions — particularly the females with young. For all we know, they may decide to attack; and they have formidable teeth.

Shark cages are not easy to handle in heavy seas. It took over thirty minutes for our launches to get them into the water. Michel Deloire immediately climbed into one of them and began filming below the surface. When the sea lions in the water showed no sign of aggressiveness, he left the cage and began shooting in the open water, without protection. The sea lions were all around him, curious, circling, but nonetheless wary. At the slightest movement from Deloire, they fled. He tried offering them live fish, caught especially for them, but it was no use. They refused to take food from his hand, even when he offered them a mackerel.

Our first encounter with the sea lions in the water counts only as a half-success, in that we were unable to establish real contact with them. Moreover, with all the kelp, the water was somewhat cloudy.

While Deloire was attempting to put together a sequence below the surface, Goupil was looking for subjects on shore. By luck, he came across a baby sea lion, nursing, and managed to get close to the mother and her offspring without frightening them. He got some excellent footage of the scene.

I must say that we are quite taken with our sea lions. It's impossible not to admire their posturing on land and their marvelous agility in the water. Our only regret is that their habitat has such an offensive odor. There are times when it is actually nauseating.

March 1. In spite of a very strong wind, we used our zodiac to film sea lions getting into the water in a large group — at least fifty specimens at once. Then, the weather worsened, and the zodiac was forced to give it up. It is impossible to do any more work today. It is 4:30 P.M., and we are going to have to put into Capetown again.

March 2. We are still at Capetown, immobilized by the weather. There were sea lions swimming around us in the port this morning, as though to shame us for being afraid of the rough water. Faced by their silent reproach, we decided to try working. We weighed anchor and managed to go a short distance. The wind was blowing at forty knots, and it was impossible to do anything. We were forced to return to port.

March 3. We left Capetown this morning to undertake a series of tests on the watertightness of our diving saucers and, if we can, to shoot some footage among the algae.

We headed first toward False Bay, but, midway, we decided to drop anchor in a cove where we would be sheltered from the wind and the waves.

We were able to get some footage of our divers among the kelps. We also found some small lobsters among the algae in the open water.

The water was ice cold. "As cold," Bonnici says, "as the water was during Precontinent III."

We tested our diving saucers at three hundred feet. They seemed in good shape.

The Wreck

Gary Haselau, a friend of ours at Capetown, had told us about a sunken ship in this area, and we decided to have a look at it. It is the *Maori*, a vessel from the First World War. The ship has been taken over entirely by kelp, and it is buried in a mass of vegetation which rises toward the surface like the branches of a tree. When one approaches the bulk from above, the effect is fantastic.

The *Maori* is inhabited by lampreys and lobsters, as Christian Bonnici and Raymond Coll discovered when they undertook a detailed inspection of the old ship. They also found a quantity of bottles, with their stoppers still in place, which they brought back to *Calypso*. We removed some of the stoppers, and we all took rather hesitant samplings of the contents. It was not bad. Not excellent, but certainly drinkable. Opinions differed on the nature of the contents. Raymond Coll thinks that it was a mixture of beer and whiskey, which is a favorite drink of the South Africans. To me, it tasted very much like beer with a high content of alcohol — probably stout. We let the bottles sit in the sun of *Calypso*'s rear deck as we compared our opinions. Suddenly there was a loud "pop," and the liquid — whatever it was — shot out of one of the bottles and drenched a section of bulkhead. After a few seconds, we noticed that the paint was beginning to peel from that section. We couldn't help wondering what this sixty-year-old beer, or whiskey, was doing to the linings of our stomachs.

Sea lions seem to enjoy spending part of their time among the breakers

Right: Raymond Coll (left) and Albert Falco make their first attempt to capture one of the animals

Sea lions are cautious creatures. They flee as soon as we try to approach them

The next morning, we planned to get some footage of the *Maori*. The kelps, which rise from the ship like ghostly hair, seemed excellent material for a few frames. Deloire was busily filming one of our divers when a group of ten South African divers arrived. Within a few minutes, the *Maori* was transformed from a sunken ship into a city being pillaged. Bottles, stacks of plates, and lobster were hauled up to the surface. The divers even took some rolls of old linoleum, which were part of the ship's cargo that we had discovered. I can't imagine why. There seems little chance that it can still be used.

The water is still icy, about 45°. By the time the divers climbed aboard the launches for the return trip to *Calypso,* they were shivering with cold. They were wearing the thin neoprene suits which we use in the Red Sea, and these are apparently inadequate for the water here.

At 1 P.M., our two launches left the area of the sunken ship to return to *Calypso.* On the way, an enormous wave caught them astern and tossed them about violently, filling the small craft with water. Bébert's boat was capsized and everyone was thrown overboard. It was also carrying two generators, which we use to run our floodlights beneath the surface, and they sank like rocks into the dense growth of kelp.

Bonnici was the only man who was able to stay in his boat. The others all ended up in the water — along with their equipment — and the surface was littered with gloves, masks, and diving suits. Our air tanks sank to the bottom.

Fortunately, the launches were well within sight of *Calypso* when the wave struck, and a rescue team was sent out immediately. It took about two hours, in forty feet of water, to recover our equipment and get it back to *Calypso.* The sea was very rough, and it was hard work, but the main problem was finding the pieces of equipment in the dense kelp. I don't think anyone will have trouble getting to sleep tonight.

Our chief mechanic immediately stripped down the two outboard motors entirely and put them back into working condition. They were running again by late afternoon. Marcelin and Jouas also began working on the generators, but that job is going to take more time than the outboards. *Calypso* is fortunate to have men whose talents go far beyond diving.

An Encounter at 300 Feet

During the next few days the weather was really impossible, and there was a very heavy swell. We decided that it would be better not to attempt to do any diving. The near loss of our two launches taught us an object lesson.

It was not until March 10 that we anchored *Calypso* in a sheltered area known as Sandy Bay and lowered our diving saucers into the water. At 1 P.M., Bébert climbed into one of them and closed the hood. As skillful a pilot as he is, the condition of the sea made it almost impossible for him to maneuver the craft. Moreover, the water was shallow and cloudy. We therefore hauled the saucer back aboard *Calypso* and then made for deeper water.

By late afternoon, the sea seemed to have settled down a bit, and we put Falco and his saucer back into the water, at a spot where it was about three hundred feet deep. The water was still rather cloudy, loaded with particles in suspension. Bébert calls it "pea soup." And, in the headlights of the saucer, it does in fact look like a heavy fog.

Bébert saw no fish. At the bottom, there were a few sponges and hydrozoa. A curious sea lion decided to inspect Bébert's vehicle at about 300 feet. This was not the first time that the animals had come — sometimes singly, sometimes in groups — to visit a minisub. They always begin by circling around, coming quite close to the saucer. Then they go down to the bottom and trail their whiskers over the sand or mud. Every time I see them, I wonder what they could possibly be searching for down there. I still do not know the answer.

The sea lions seemed perfectly comfortable at a depth of 300 feet.* We generally see them in great numbers at depths of 125 or 150 feet.

Their performance around the diving saucer increased our curiosity and our sympathy. It is fascinating to watch them move with such speed and grace in deep water as they maneuver around the saucer. I have the feeling that our adventure with sea lions is just beginning.

March 11. There was a thick fog almost all day. We cruised about, looking for an area where the water was relatively clear, but without success. Finally, at about 3:30 P.M., conditions seemed more favorable. We immediately lowered two saucers into the water, with Falco at the controls of one and André Laban in the other. Both saucers circled around, executing various maneuvers and filming each other with the marine cameras which are built into them.

At 5 P.M., it began to rain, and the sea grew heavier. Using our marine telephone, I advised Falco and Laban to return immediately to *Calypso*. A few minutes later, we hoisted the saucers aboard — which, in a rough sea, requires acrobatic dexterity.

---

*The Navy Undersea Center in San Diego has run tests and concluded that the sea lions have much greater depth capabilities than 300 feet.

One of the sea lions — the one we will name Pepito — has just been captured . . .

. . . and the other one, the future Christobald, tries desperately to escape the same fate

March 12. There is still a heavy swell from the southwest. I am beginning to be a bit concerned about our schedule. There is so much to do, and the continuing bad weather has put us far behind in our work. I had hoped that we would be able to continue our observation of sea lions. I had even thought that we might be able to shoot an entire film on sea lions. There are no longer many places where they are as numerous as here at the Cape. In the past 250 years, they have been hunted relentlessly for their oil and their hides, and the sea lion population of the world has declined from several millions to a few hundred thousand. They have enemies in addition to man: sharks, and especially killer whales.

The decreasing number of sea lions is a tragedy. They are truly remarkable animals, with well-developed minds. The brain of the sea lion is larger than that of the dog, though smaller than that of the porpoise.

Every year, the sea lions cross vast stretches of ocean to return to their place of birth. The large males — they sometimes weigh over 650 pounds — are quite aggressive, and they are "lords of the beach." They surround themselves with harems of numerous females, and, as soon as a female has given birth to a calf (which weighs from twelve to fourteen pounds), she again mates with the male. The female bears only one young at a time, and she gives birth in the year following the mating.

Unfortunately, we will now have to cut short our study of the furred sea lions of the Cape. We are all — *Calypso* and her teams, as well as myself — burdened with an overambitious schedule. We have work in the New World, where we are expected to open up a new archaeological dig in the Caribbean, in a bank of coral, which has never been done before.[1] We want to dive in Lake Titicaca[2] in the Andes, at an altitude of 13,000 feet, in order to gather data on the physiological effects of diving at such an altitude; and there are a half-dozen projects, including some films, that we must begin work on very shortly.

I am not very enthusiastic about the prospect of *Calypso*'s crossing the Atlantic in the middle of the hurricane season. It seems to me a questionable use of men and material. Moreover, we are all disappointed at having to give up on the sea lions so quickly. Our teams are quite taken with these animals. What is the solution? Perhaps we should consider capturing one or two of the animals and keeping them aboard *Calypso*. We could then study them at

[1]See *Diving for Sunken Treasure*, by Jacques-Yves Cousteau and Philippe Diolé, Doubleday & Co., Inc., Garden City, and Cassell, London, 1972.

[2]See *Three Adventures*, by Jacques-Yves Cousteau and Philippe Diolé, Doubleday & Co., Inc., Garden City, and *Galápagos—Titicaca—The Blue Holes,* by Jacques-Yves Cousteau and Philippe Diolé, Cassell, London, 1973.

Pepito is wrapped in a net and taken back to the launch

Right: Aboard *Calypso*, our new guest has now regained his composure and is attending to his toilette

leisure. It would be an exciting experience. Still, this is a solution that I am reluctant to propose. I don't like the idea of removing animals from their natural environment, especially marine mammals like these, who are so obviously attached to their freedom and so active in the water. And I like even less the idea of training and conditioning animals and teaching them "tricks," as people do in zoos and circuses. Yet, there is a truly exciting aspect of the idea. What if we were to capture two sea lions and leave them to themselves as much as we could? They seem genuinely curious about our men. Would they then become accustomed to the presence of humans? Would they perhaps follow our divers in the depths of the sea, the way that dogs follow their masters for a walk through the woods?

A Case of Conscience

The question of taking sea lions captive has been on my mind for some time. I have asked myself to what extent man's urge to accustom animals to his own way of living is actually an unnatural, or rather an anti-nature, attitude. It seems to me that it is basically symptomatic of man's desire for approval by animals.

In this whole affair of the sea lions, I have given much thought to this case of conscience because I am really eager to *know* sea lions, and to find out whether it is possible for us to make anything out of them other than circus animals. If it is not possible, then it would surely be wrong for us even to consider capturing a pair of them. But from what we have observed, it may be that they could actually become our diving partners rather than mere "performers."

If we admit the working principle that sea lions can be associated to certain human enterprises — I do not necessarily mean that we must admit the moral principle, which is something else again — it follows that they can render a number of very practical services to us. At the time, I was thinking particularly of our experience during our three unsuccessful attempts to explain the Vaucluse fountain. Each time, we had managed to go a little deeper. The third time, we had gone deeper than previously, by sending down our telenaut (a remote-controlled marine camera) below the level where we were. But even the telenaut came to a halt at a depth of 375 feet, though we were almost certain that the well went deeper than that. I think that, in such a situation, a sea lion could have been of real service to us — more so than a dolphin because the sea lion is more supple and is accustomed to maneuvering in places where the dolphin would scrape the skin from its body and go into panic. It is even possible that a sea lion might have been able to dive with an automatic camera strapped to its back and return with precious information on the dark maze into which it is now impossible for humans to venture.

These are all factors which I weighed carefully. Then, I ordered *Calypso* on a course toward Seal Island, the home of the sea lions. I had decided that we would try to capture two of the animals. I gave the divers detailed instructions, emphasizing that the sea lions were to be handled with the utmost care and gentleness and that they were to be taken in such a way as to avoid frightening them. Yet I must admit that my conscience was not wholly at ease. It goes against the grain to deprive animals of their liberty, no matter how worthy our motives may be. It is useless to pretend that captivity in any form is less than cruel.

By 2 P.M., we were moored off Seal Island. Through my binoculars, I saw the waves breaking violently against the shore; and, with an emptiness in the pit of my stomach, I saw the brown and reddish shapes of the sea lions on their accustomed rocks, their small round heads stretched out toward the sun. . . .

At four o'clock we were ready, and a first launch started for shore carrying two cameramen accompanied by Dr. Millet, Dominique Sumian, and Yves Omer. Next, the zodiac left, with Bébert, Falco, Raymond Coll, Michel Deloire, Christian Bonnici; then, the second launch, with André Laban, Maurice Léandri, and René Haon. I had decided to use the largest number of personnel possible, so as to obtain the best results in the shortest time. I hoped that we could still get in a few days of filming and perhaps even shoot the capture itself. Then, while making the Atlantic crossing, we would film further sequences and thus end up with a complete record of our experience with the captive sea lions.

The launches were tossed about violently in the waves, and the zodiac was caught in the swift undertow which surrounds the island. The situation was made doubly dangerous by the rocks in the area. Bébert tried to disembark at the northeastern point of the island, where there are broad, flat stretches of rock, but he discovered that they were covered with algae and extremely slippery. Michel Deloire jumped onto the rocks after Bébert but lost his footing and fell. He was unable to rise, and his right foot was extremely painful. He called Dr. Millet by walkie-talkie, and the doctor used our second zodiac to rush to the scene. It was immediately evident to him that Michel had fractured a bone in his foot. He would have to be evacuated; and, at the same time, it was important that he be moved as little as possible. He would also have to be taken to Capetown the next day for X rays and a cast.

A large number of sea lions were visible both on the beach and in the water. The raucous cries of the latter, and their gamboling in the water, were in surprising contrast to the tranquility of the older, and no doubt wiser, animals which, lying on the rocks and basking in the sun, reacted to our arrival only by craning their necks in our direction.

The calm was of brief duration. The first time we tried to throw our net over a sea lion, it fled, giving the alarm. Immediately all the other animals took fright and fled to the stone slabs on the western shore of the island, so as to be able to dive into the sea.

Meanwhile, our men were in full pursuit of our sea lion, with four divers carrying the open net. All but one man slipped and fell on the slippery rock. And the sure-footed member of the team got caught in the net and joined his friends on the ground.

While this drama was being played out with the net team, Dominique

Sumian tried to herd one of the animals into a spot where it could be captured. He was so busy with his intended captive that he did not see another sea lion lunge at him. The animal sank its teeth into what would have been the flesh of Dominique's thigh if it had not been for his diving suit. The suits were uncomfortable in the heat, but not entirely useless.

As Laban and Lionel manned the cameras and Marcelin worked the tape recorder, a sea lion was finally taken prisoner without being handled too roughly. We now faced the second part of the problem: how to get the animal aboard *Calypso*. Our plan was to tie the net containing the animal to a wooden pole, which would then be carried on Sumian and Bonnici's shoulders out to one of the launches. The trouble was that it was impossible to get through the breakers while carrying this heavy load. Falco then ran a line between shore and the launch, to which René and Maurice attached the net preparatory to shuttling the sea lion out to the waiting boat. At that moment, however, a lengthy debate arose over this method of transportation. Everyone was concerned that the sea lion might suffocate in the tight net, or be hurt before it reached the launch. Our solicitude was not without a basis in reality. The water was extremely rough, and our small boats were dancing like corks in the waves. Yet, Falco's line, which was really quite secure, was the only method available; and it was finally decided to try it, with the exercise of infinite care. It worked. There were none of the mishaps that we had all feared. The divers then gathered their equipment and, slipping and falling on the rocks, got it all out to their boats. There was a session of petting the sea lion before putting it safely into one of the shark cages. It had survived the ordeal of capture and transportation; but it did seem a bit shaken by the experience.

Family Life

A good part of the sea lion's time is spent in the water. Sea lion mothers sometimes remain in the sea for several days before returning to land to nurse their young. At the time that we were on Seal Island, the young appeared to be about two months old, and the inland pools on the island were dotted with their little black heads.

Dr. Millet was responsible for studying the life-style of sea lions on land, and he made a number of useful observations. "When a man approaches one of the pools where the young are swimming," he reports, "the mothers leave. There are usually 150 or 200 young in each of the pools, so there is a correspondingly large number of mothers in attendance. The pools, it seems, are

The Zodiac makes a farewell tour of Seal Island

the nurseries of the sea lions. It's my opinion, however, that some of the mothers stay close to one or the other of the small animals. I have no way of knowing whether these are the weakest of the young, or simply the favorites.

"Along with the divers, I have been able to observe the young rather closely. They have a difficult life in the midst of the constant agitation of the harem of adults. They are born with their eyes open, and they are already furred at birth. They nurse at irregular intervals and they take several liters of milk at a single nursing. Between nursing sessions, they teach themselves to swim, first in the pools of water left by the tide, then, later, in the sea.

"It is fairly easy to approach sleeping sea lions. All one has to do is to move upwind. It appears that, when the animals are asleep, the olfactory sense is the one that is the most alert. Moving upwind, one can come to within three feet of a sleeping sea lion. But as soon as it sees you, it flees. It seems that it reacts most strongly to what it sees."

Dr. Millet's observations were confirmed by the experience of the men attempting to capture a second sea lion. As soon as Bonnici, Falco, Coll, and the others tried to get close enough to an animal to throw their net over it, not only the individual sea lion but the whole herd of them fled in panic.

Bébert tried throwing the net, gladiator-style, but by the time it struck the ground, the target sea lion was far away. Several other methods were tried, with similar lack of success. The rocks tore the nets and, when the nets were wet, they were too heavy to be handled. It was like a French comedy, if I may use that expression, with everyone running around shouting, slipping on excrement, laughing, and trying new tricks.

Seen from *Calypso*'s deck, through binoculars, the antics of our team were irresistibly funny. Since the divers themselves seemed to be having such a good time, I did not feel guilty about laughing at their misadventures. The most comical aspect of the situation was that, of the two sides, the sea lions seemed the superior. They moved quickly and with assurance over the slippery rocks, while our men — as accustomed as they are to jumping from rock to rock — were spending most of their time flat on their backs on the slippery algae.

In any event, the sea lions mounted a spirited resistance to our aggressive designs. And with their seventy-five pounds of muscle and their pointed teeth, they were not adversaries to be taken lightly. Even so, it had never occurred to us that they could be so agile.

It was Dominique Sumian who finally developed a successful tactic. He reached out with his massive arms and grabbed a sea lion from behind, by its hind paws. Immediately, Raymond Coll threw a net over it, and the animal was immobilized. The net was then hooked to a pole and attached to a line from the launch. The launch carried the animal to *Calypso,* where it was housed temporarily in a second antishark cage.

We now had our two sea lions.

But not for long. During the night, the second animal escaped. René was taking a shower and saw it loose on the rear deck. He rushed out, naked, but he was too late. The sea lion had already dived into the water.

No one was happy about the prospect of having to begin again the next day. Before going to sleep, we wrapped a net around the shark cage which still contained the first sea lion.

March 15. We sent another team out to the island this morning. Our technique had now been perfected, and almost immediately Sumian had his hands on a sea lion. The animal was quickly netted, hooked to the line, and ferried out to *Calypso.* For the moment, however, we are keeping it out of sight of the first captured animal.

We are running out of time. Today, we completed tests on a new apparatus, developed by Commandant Alinat, which the divers insist on calling "the wheelbarrow." It is a trailer to which a camera has been attached, and it was designed to be towed by a launch. We hope that eventually it will enable us to get shots of whales while they are moving. There are still one or two "bugs" to be ironed out. When the diver riding on the trailer attempts to work its rudder, the wheelbarrow tends to spin (and so does the diver).

After the tests, we returned to Capetown. We are very worried about our two sea lions. So far, they have refused to eat. If this keeps up, we will have to release them.

Nonetheless, they seem in good health. They are both quite young and probably males. One is grayish, and the other reddish-brown. They both appear to be more or less resigned to the experience that we are imposing on them. Even so, we have to be on our guard against the bites which they lavish on us with such prodigality.

Bébert dived into the water and came back clutching a couple of live sea bream. He quickly fileted them and held the filets out to the sea lions. Without a moment's hesitation, they gulped down the fish.

Bonnici repeated Bébert's performance, and again the sea lions ate the fish eagerly. We seem to have solved the first problem with our sea lions.

March 18 and 19. We have been busy getting our sea lions installed on *Calypso*'s rear deck. We bought a blue plastic pool for them, and Dominique Sumian has built a wooden framework to hold it in place. The two shark cages open directly onto the pool. And, to forestall any more escapes, we have covered the whole thing with a net. As soon as the pool was filled, the sea lions dived in with every sign of delight. They swam around eagerly, twisting and jumping until the entire rear deck was awash from their splashing.

When they had calmed down a bit, Michel Bernard undertook to give them a bath with the hose and a brush. The two animals seem to enjoy being washed and groomed.

We have assigned a diver to look after each of the animals. Michel Bernard is to care for the larger animal, the gray one, which has already been named Christobald. And Raymond Coll has an obvious affection for the younger one and will look after it. He has already christened it Pepito. We are on the threshold of new friendships, and our sentimental adventure is beginning.

I think that, with sufficient care and affection, Pepito and Christobald will accustom themselves to life aboard *Calypso* and will be able to live happily among us. Yet, I feel no better about the fact that we are holding these animals captive and forcing them to submit to an experiment.

We are going to have certain logistical problems because of the animals.

Pepito decides that *Calypso*'s aft deck is ideal for sunbathing

For example, we are going to have to provide food for them during the three weeks that it will take for us to cross the Atlantic. I will have to buy a refrigerator for them at Capetown, and about a hundred and fifty pounds of sardines.

Actually, sea lions are able to go for two weeks without eating, when food is lacking, thanks to their store of fat. When food is plentiful, however, an adult may eat daily from fifteen to twenty pounds of fish, squid, and crustaceans.

March 21. Today we began our transatlantic voyage. Our ultimate destination is Natal, in Brazil. En route, we will call at St. Helena and at Ascension Isle.

If we are lucky, the good weather will hold.

Two

Pepito and Christobald

March 23, 1967. We are two days out of the Cape of Good Hope, and the weather is beautiful. If our luck holds, my guess is that we will put into Natal, and then make for the Caribbean, sometime in mid-April.

Pepito and Christobald are gradually becoming accustomed to their life among humans aboard a boat where there is not enough room for all the men, let alone for two sea lions. Nonetheless, we must make every effort to provide them with the best living conditions that we can. They spend almost 80 per cent of their time in the sea. Also, we have built them a real swimming pool out of laminated plywood lined with blue vinyl. Before leaving the Cape, we had covered the hatch of the aft hold with a net for them; now, there are three new areas, covered with canvas, which are much more spacious. We have also devised a system which circulates sea water in the pool, in order to protect Pepito and Christobald against heat and dehydration.

We live in dread that they will get caught in the mesh of the nets, and I have arranged a schedule so that they will be watched twenty-four hours a day. We have installed a television camera over their pool for this purpose.

The waves present another problem. They are sometimes so high that there is always the danger that the water will be spilled from the pool and that the two sea lions will be hurled against the nets.

Our worries apparently are not shared by Pepito and Christobald. They seem delighted with their new equipment, and they cavort in their pool as though they were still at the Cape. Yet, they refuse to eat the frozen fish that we bought for them before leaving Capetown. They have not eaten, in fact, since Falco fed them his filets of sea bream.

We are intrigued by the sounds they make, and it is frustrating not to know what they signify. If we could learn to interpret at least one of them, it would be a beginning of communication, which would lead to a beginning of trust. We have heard them make a noise from their throats, like a bark, but we are unable to guess what it means. It may be defiance, or a warning. This morning, we also heard a deeper cry, and we have no idea what it signified.

The only thing of which we are certain is that Pepito and Christobald are enjoying their pool, and it is a delight to watch them playing in their natural element. Yet, the amount of water that we can provide is quite small, and we can only guess what these animals are like when they have the boundless sea for their games.

They spend a certain amount of time grooming themselves. Their snouts are the object of much attention, and they use one of their hind legs to scratch themselves.

The Clothesline

March 24. Our chief worry now is to get Pepito and Christobald interested in eating, especially Christobald, who seems to be the ringleader. He eats nothing at all, yet he seems to be in good health. Obviously, he is living off of his reserves of fat, but he is very young, and I can't believe that he will be able to do so much longer.

Pepito does not eat either, but he entertains us constantly. He chews on a fish for a while, then throws it into the air or out of the pool. The larger the audience, the more stunts he performs. His tricks have earned him the nickname of "the Clown." When he is particularly devilish, we call him Pepito the Dunce.

Raymond Coll has developed a real affection for Pepito, just as teachers sometimes tend to do with particularly mischievous pupils.

Today, we tried a new method of inducing the sea lions to eat. We installed a double line on pulleys over the pool, and then attached a fish to the line, which we moved back and forth (temptingly, we hoped) over the water. Pepito grabbed the fish, then let it fall into the pool. We tried raising the fish higher, but the same thing happened again. The clothesline method was a failure, but the animals seemed to enjoy the game. At least we are amusing them, and perhaps that is making their captivity easier to bear.

Next, we tried a modification of the plan. We took the stool, which Gaston uses to climb into the diving saucer, and then hung the fish high over it. Then we began shaking the fish. It took about five minutes for Pepito to understand the game. He jumped up on the stool, grabbed the fish, began chewing it — and spat out the pieces.

We are beginning to feel a little discouraged.

The Personalities

March 28. We have now been at sea for eight days and Pepito and Christobald still have eaten nothing. It is not because we have not tried. Bonnici and Sumian get into the pool, move the fish over the surface of the water, push it toward the sea lions' little pointed teeth — and sometimes Pepito and Christobald rip it out of their hands. "Good," we say. "It's working. They're going to eat." Then, they let the pieces of fish fall back into the water. After several attempts of this kind, there were twelve or fifteen pounds of fish lying on the bottom, and we had to clean the pool.

We have noted something peculiar. Christobald is trying to establish his authority in the pool by making life difficult for Pepito. When we try to feed the animals — which we do at the same time every day — Christobald rushes in and grabs the fish. He doesn't eat it, but he will not let Pepito have it. It is possible that, if it were not for Christobald, Pepito would eat.

The personalities of the two sea lions are beginning to emerge, and they are quite distinct. Pepito is the more affectionate of the two. One might even say that he is becoming attached to Raymond Coll. Moreover, he is very playful. Christobald is not as gentle and is certainly more wary of humans, but he has more vitality and perhaps more intelligence than Pepito.

Today, eleven days after capturing the sea lions, I am in a better position to foresee the road that we will have to travel before arriving at a relationship of mutual understanding and trust with these marine mammals, which are not so very different from ourselves in size, and whose psychology, I suspect, is akin to our own.

What I am particularly on guard against is the temptation to turn them into "trained animals." That is not our purpose; it cannot be. If it were, it would have been wrong to capture them in the first place. For that reason, I have ordered the use of the stool to be discontinued in our attempts to feed

Our dog, Zoom, tries to strike up a friendship with Pepito; but Pepito is more interested in grooming his whiskers than in making new friends

Pepito and Christobald, although it is true that Pepito learned to climb up onto the stool by himself and that the fish, since it is not eaten, is only a symbolic reward for a trick performed.

How difficult it is to allow our sea lions to exercise their spontaneity aboard a boat like this one. Perhaps I am being utopian in my refusal to allow Pepito and Christobald to be deformed. After all, they must learn to live aboard *Calypso,* surrounded by thirty men. To tell the truth, I am a bit concerned about their tricks and their strutting. I have a strange impression that Pepito and Christobald are interested in us and in the opinion that we are forming of them. It occurs to me that animals often work at surprising humans. That, however, is still only a vague impression.

Nonetheless, I must say that if Pepito and Christobald are well disposed toward us, their benevolence is only relative. They still bite us frequently. Even though we have all learned to be on our guard, their teeth often are on target. Dr. Millet is kept busy caring for these bites, with everything from Band-Aids to stitches. The bite of a sea lion is not much less serious than that, say, of a small bear.

Pepito and Christobald swim around continuously, despite the narrowness of their pool. We were greatly impressed by their gracefulness in the water

The problem of Pepito and Christobald's excrement is almost of as much concern to us as that of their food. The smell of Seal Island was overwhelming. It is not less so here. It is difficult to teach them habits of cleanliness, as one can do so easily with dogs or cats. The sea lions are immaculate so far as they themselves are concerned, but everything around them is a mess. We are constantly at work cleaning the rear deck and the pool.

I was hoping that our dog, Zoom, a bloodhound much loved aboard *Calypso,* would provide some interesting data, either by making friends with the sea lions or by becoming their enemy. But there is not much to be learned from what has happened so far. When Zoom came to sniff his new shipmates, Pepito's whiskers rose, but he showed no other signs of hostility. Christobald, however, is more aggressive, and he tried to bite Zoom's nose. Zoom moved away just in the nick of time, and, obviously disappointed and angry, he retired to the foredeck. Since then, he has been sulking. The rear deck had always been his domain before the arrival of the sea lions, and he obviously resents their presence. However, I know he is too gentle a dog to start a fight with the newcomers. I wish I had as much confidence in Christobald.

A First Meeting

In about two weeks, we will reach St. Helena, our first port of call. The weather continues to be beautiful.

I would like very much for Pepito and Christobald to be sufficiently tame to have the run of *Calypso* — under surveillance, of course. I think the time has come for us to undertake a gradual and calculated *rapprochement* between man and sea lion. This is perhaps too much to expect from animals which are still ready to bite at the least provocation. It is also perhaps too much to ask of the men who are going to be bitten.

The sea lions seem to have gotten over their fear of us, but they have not yet reached the stage of co-operation. They have gone through the noisy stage, and they are now in the lethargic stage. There are no more games in the pool, no more stunts with the fish. Both Pepito and Christobald seem totally indifferent to everything around them. Pepito sits in the sun and spends most of his time grooming himself. It is worth noting, however, that sometimes he allows us to pet him.

A week ago, on the rear deck, we arranged a large enclosure, surrounded by netting, for the animals. They now have much more room to move about. However, we are not sure that they could not get out of the enclosure if they tried; so, at night, we return them to their shark cages, and every morning we let them out into the enclosure. This arrangement will also allow us to separate Pepito and Christobald at mealtime; and perhaps Pepito, once he is free of Christobald's influence, will begin to eat.

March 31. Today, Michel Bernard, wearing thick gloves, boots, and chaps (which we had made in Capetown), had a confrontation with Christobald. We had no intention of beginning to train the sea lion in any way. What we wanted was for Christobald to allow himself to be petted and to get over his aggressive demonstrations.

Christobald, as I have already mentioned, is the more "difficult" of the two sea lions. That is not hard to understand. He is slightly older than Pepito, and he has had more experience with freedom. Also, he is practically an adult, which means that he is too old to seek human contact in the way that immature animals do when they are separated from their parents. In spite of Christobald's apparently hostile temperament, we have decided to surround him with affection in the hope of eliciting a related response.

The first meeting between Michel Bernard and Christobald ended in a draw. Michel managed to pet Christobald's flanks, and even to stroke his head; but Christobald countered by tearing off the top of a glove and biting an ankle which, fortunately, was encased in tough leather.

Michel Bernard, wearing his "armor," tries to come to terms with Christobald

Pepito, on the other hand, is much more affectionate with Raymond Coll. To be sure, he shows his teeth from time to time, but Raymond talks to him, pets him, and calms him. It is obvious that the human voice has a decided effect upon the sea lions. It doesn't really matter what one says, since it is the sound itself which seems to tranquilize them and inspire confidence. Yet, their ears are very small, and their sense of hearing is not particularly well developed.

Sessions between Pepito and Raymond always end with the sea lion getting a bath and brushing, which Pepito enjoys enormously.

Success

We have concluded that our frozen fish simply is not very appetizing to the sea lions. In fact, its soft texture and shredded flesh is rather disgusting.

Neither Pepito nor Christobald has eaten for thirteen days now. Since they are taking no nourishment, they have begun to conserve their strength as much as possible. They are now swimming at might and remaining motionless during the day.

We have heard, for the second time, the deep cry that we heard shortly after their capture. Is it a sound of distress?

The animals love the sun, and they would lie in it all day if, when the heat is particularly bad, we did not force them into the pool.

The enclosure, which we sprinkle throughout the day, is their favorite spot. They lie there, their eyes half-closed but nonetheless watchful. Sometimes they rise, to see if the way to the sea is open at last. When they do so, we watch with particular care, for we know what they are thinking. When we see their eyes open wide and their whiskers rise, we know that they are planning to act. Their whiskers are extremely mobile and almost invariably reveal their emotions.

Coll and Bonnici have succeeded in measuring the sea lions with the help of Michel Bernard who, for the occasion, wore his leather gloves and chaps.

A few days ago, we began using a bell in our efforts to get the animals to

Right: Jamestown valley, on St. Helena

Michel Bernard tries to persuade Christobald to climb up on a stool

eat. Every evening, the frozen fish is put out on deck to defrost. In the morning, before leading the animals out onto the rear deck for their meal (which they never eat), we ring the ship's bell. They know quite well that the bell means breakfast, but that knowledge does not increase their appetite.

April 1. This morning, Pepito and Christobald *ate.* We encountered a school of flying fish; or rather, we ran into a swarm of them. They crashed against *Calypso*'s hull, and many of them landed on the rear deck. The sea lions were unbelievably excited and threw themselves on all of the fish within their reach. We gathered up all the rest and gave them to Pepito and Christobald.

Christobald still has the bad habit of grabbing everything that we offer to Pepito.

St. Helena

April 4. We have been at sea for fifteen days now, without seeing either land or another ship. We have had sun for almost the entire time and a fairly good sea. The teams have had a good rest after their hard work at the Cape.

Every day we have what I call our "friendship sessions" with the sea lions, which last one hour. These are in addition to the time that we spend with them as individuals. Everyone on board has gotten into the habit of talking to Pepito and Christobald in gentle, affectionate tones, and this practice is beginning to have its effect. I think that very soon we are going to reach a new stage in our relationship and that the sea lions are going to be able to have more freedom aboard *Calypso.* However, I do not want to attempt anything like this until we have left St. Helena. In fact, while we are in port, we will have to double our guard to make sure there are no escapes.

I am beginning to sound like a prison warden, a role which I find particularly distasteful. I'm sure many people would think it strange that the plight of a couple of sea lions could plague my conscience. Perhaps it is because of where we are. In the distance, I can see the island of St. Helena, which was surely once the most famous prison in the world. Here, Sir Hudson Lowe stood guard over the fallen Emperor Napoleon. . . .

St. Helena looks as one would expect it to look. It rises from the sea like a fortress, an enormous ocher rock in the sun. We arrived in the late afternoon, and we glimpsed what appeared to be a black fault in the rock: the only large street on the island, lined with houses.

It is impossible to dock a vessel even the size of *Calypso* at St. Helena. We moored offshore and went in by zodiac. Even then, it was not easy to disem-

Pepito is much more sociable than Christobald

bark. The pier was being repaired, and we had to climb ashore by means of a rope hanging from a gate. Tourists must be quite athletic to visit St. Helena.*

It was a Sunday when we arrived, and we saw no one. The town seemed deserted. There was life only in the church, from which we heard the sound of youthful voices singing a hymn. Bernard Chauvelin and Dr. Millet entered the building, and their intrusion threw a choir of twenty-five young girls, all in white, into utter confusion. The hymn was not resumed until the choirmaster,

*I understand that the pier has now (1973) been repaired.

Yves Omer is obviously Pepito's favorite

Right: Friends napping: Michel Bernard and Christobald

a clergyman in regulation black, rapped sharply twice with his baton.

The landing party ended up in the town's only pub, drinking beer in an atmosphere of unrelieved depression.

A Miraculous Catch

Meanwhile, friends of Pepito and Christobald who had remained aboard *Calypso* were very busy. Bonnici and Coll were preparing, when it grew dark, for a Mediterranean-style *lamparo* fishing. Following the lamparo system, a large light was lowered into the water, and, very soon, there was a school of mackerel following closely on *Calypso*'s stern. Everyone fished with lines and *salabres*, and there was a magnificent catch. In no time at all, we had

taken several pounds of fish, which were immediately divided between Pepito and Christobald. "They ate," Bonnici says, "as though they were on the verge of starvation. The fish disappeared down their throats as though by magic."

When the sea lions had had enough, the fishing continued until there was a sufficient supply of fresh fish to fill the sea lions' freezer. The frozen fish we had bought at Capetown was thrown away, to everyone's relief. From now on, Pepito and Christobald would at least have appetizing meals.

An Official Visit

Within the next few days, *Calypso* received an official visit from the governor of St. Helena, and his lady. The governor's wife was eager to explore

Calypso, but she was wearing high heels which were not designed for climbing around on shipboard. Dr. Millet resolved the impasse by providing a pair of low-heeled sandals in an appropriate size. During the tour of the ship, Pepito and Christobald were much admired. They behaved more or less properly before our visitors.

Later, there was a reception at Government House, and then a tour in the governor's Rolls-Royce to the high plateau of the island, where the vegetation contrasts strikingly with the aridity of the rest of the rock. We also visited Longwood, Napoleon's residence on St. Helena, where a diplomat, who is also a well-known historian, gave us a lecture as fascinating as it was impromptu.

Dr. Millet spent his time at the local hospital, as he always does at ports of call. He is never so happy as when he is able to be of assistance to a medical confrere. Thanks to this practice of his, *Calypso* always has a more than adequate store of medical supplies which we, in turn, share with anyone in need.

On this occasion, Dr. Millet's arrival was particularly welcome at the hospital. A South Korean ship had put into St. Helena some two weeks earlier, and there had been an outbreak of venereal disease. The chief medical officer at the hospital was at wit's end because the disease was resistant to all the drugs he had on hand — news which Dr. Millet gleefully imparted to *Calypso*'s men. He also reported that the local population was not remarkable for good health, and that the people were constantly subject to disease and to alcoholism.

During our walks on the island, we encountered a couple about sixty years old who had never once been to the town, which was about ten miles away. The couple were of mixed English and Indian blood.

Before leaving St. Helena, we dived to a sunken ship in shallow water, but it was a vessel without special interest for us and did not seem to be worth a filmed sequence. We had taken down all of our equipment for nothing.

The dive did have a serendipitous effect. It encumbered *Calypso*'s rear deck with our customary projectors, cables, and other such equipment, and disturbed the sea lions. Also, for a while everyone was busy and had no time for Pepito and Christobald. This period of being ignored — a new experience for them — seems to have strengthened the sea lions' affection for us. When we returned from the dive, they leaped at Michel Bernard, begging for fish.

They now also recognize Raymond Coll, Yves Omer, Dominique Sumian, and Christian Bonnici.

Upon leaving St. Helena, I decided to enter upon a new stage of our relationship with Pepito and Christobald by allowing them a certain amount of freedom while keeping them under observation. They were to be allowed the run of *Calypso*'s passages and foredeck, but I ordered the sea lions' adopted fathers, Michel Bernard and Raymond Coll, never to let their charges out of their sight.

Pepito is a cause of continual satisfaction to us. He follows Raymond Coll everywhere. There is an obvious bond of affection between them. Coll is a sensitive, intuitive man, and Pepito has certainly sensed this and responded to it in his own way.

There was even a rumor, couched in terms of admiration, that Pepito had, entirely on his own, managed to climb the stairwell in *Calypso*'s port passage. I do know that when Raymond Coll is at the wheel, Pepito is always with him, lying at his feet.

Christobald, on the other hand, is less of a prodigy. He sits, folding his tail under him as all sea lions do,* sniffs the wind, and wiggles his whiskers. Obviously, he longs for freedom, which is not surprising. Bernard knows very well what is going on in that small round head, and he tries to cajole Christobald by hugging and petting him and trying to make him climb upon his lap, but without much success.

Even so, it has been fully forty-eight hours since Dr. Millet has had to treat a case of sea-lion bite.

Ascension Island

We are within sight of Ascension Island, and halfway across the Atlantic. The island is a desertlike stretch of land, pierced by small craters among which rise radar towers. Ascension belongs to the British, but the Americans have a large base there which is used for launching rockets and which also plays a part in the Apollo program.

This port of call is very different from St. Helena, but it is quite interesting in its own way. We arrived at a time when there was a rehearsal underway for a launching of an Apollo shot from Cape Kennedy.

The American officers greeted us warmly and very courteously showed us their enormously complex installation, which is tied-in directly to the NASA information center at Houston, Texas. Ascension Island is one of the tracking stations after a launching has taken place from the continental United States.

---

*This is characteristic of sea lions, as distinct from seals who cannot do so because of the shape of their pelvis.

Christobald sits for his portrait. The artist: Christobald's great and good friend, Michel Bernard

Left: One of Raymond Coll's chores is to feed Pepito. He does so at the same time every day and always makes a ceremony of the occasion

Pepito keeps Raymond Coll company when Raymond is on watch

The Americans also took us on a jeep tour of the island. At the summit, there is a plateau with a fair amount of vegetation and several scattered farms. It is the only place on the island where there is rainfall. There are clouds, cottages, lawns, the governor's residence — a very British enclave, surrounded entirely by American technology.

As we were returning to the coast, the jeeps came to a halt, and our hosts pointed out a red light which had suddenly appeared above one of the craters. It was 3 P.M. less seven minutes. At precisely three o'clock, a trapdoor slid open, and, with a deafening whistle, a rocket shot out of its subterranean silo. I was told that there was one launching a day.

The very rudimentary port equipment of Ascension Island is in strange contrast to the American installation, which includes an air field. The office of the Port Captain, for example, is nothing more than a wooden shed, before which a rusted cannon stands; and the docking facilities are quite primitive.

Our American friends told us about a sunken ship near *Calypso*'s mooring, but when we visited it we were disappointed. It was nothing but scrap iron, with no interest for us. I am sure that there must be other sunken ships around Ascension. The island has been a port of call for ships in the Atlantic for the past four centuries. But we are not here to indulge our interest in archaeology. Our immediate task is to catch enough fish for our sea lions.

In that respect, our experience at St. Helena has encouraged us. We decided to try again at night. As soon as the lamp was beneath the surface, an enormous school of sardines appeared out of nowhere, next to *Calypso*'s hull. We could see their scales shimmering in the light. Once more, there was a miraculous catch. In a few minutes, Bonnici and Dr. Millet, between them, hauled in twenty-five pounds of fish. Everyone tried his luck. Ten men on deck simply tied hooks to lines and dropped them overboard, without bait.

The champion fisherman of the evening was Raymond Coll, who took the salabre down to the diving platform and lowered it into the water. Every time he did so, it filled with so many sardines that he was unable to raise it without help.

Finally, we had enough. The freezers were full, and the sea lions had sufficient food to last them until we reached the Caribbean. They were already gulping down the live, squirming fish that Bernard threw into their pool.

I should add that fishing is not an activity to which we are partial aboard *Calypso*, and we never indulge in it for our own sakes. The sea lions have made us violate one of our principles, but, in return, they will be able to eat the twenty-odd pounds of fish which are their normal daily ration.

Leaving Ascension Island on the second leg of our voyage across the

Atlantic, we are also opening a new chapter in our sea lion adventure. Now, we will have to concentrate in doing everything that we can for them to regain their strength and be in perfect health. Actually, they are eating with good appetite, and Dr. Millet is putting vitamins into the sardines he feeds them. However, as much as possible, I would like Pepito and Christobald always to be fed by the same persons: Coll for Pepito, and Bernard for Christobald. Moreover, I want mealtime to be accompanied by a rather complex ceremony. I will ask Raymond and Michel to wear their diving suits and to attach a basket to their waists containing the fish and squid they feed to the sea lions. Also, we will continue to ring the ship's bell to announce the beginning of the feeding session.

In other words, I have no intention of canceling our somewhat ambitious program. To the contrary, the progress made by Pepito, and even by Christobald, is quite encouraging. We are not trying to turn the two sea lions into shipboard pets, or mascots, but to teach them to become our diving companions. It is at the latter point that we are running the greatest risk. There is nothing to make us think that, as soon as they are in the open water, Pepito and Christobald will not escape. Their longing for freedom will very likely be stronger than any attachment they may feel for us.

Harnesses

In view of that possiblity, at Capetown I had harnesses made which buckle around the sea lions' bodies. The first few times that Pepito and Christobald go into the water with the divers, they will be on leashes. At the moment, we are trying to accustom them to harnesses. Pepito, with his usual docility, allowed the apparatus to be buckled on; Christobald was less docile but eventually submitted. The trouble came when we tried to take the animals for a stroll on their leashes around *Calypso*'s deck. For several days, they had enjoyed relative freedom, and now they were restricted in their movements. There were bites, cries, and scenes on deck and in the passages. Such things are to be expected. We cannot take an animal from its natural environment, plunge it into wholly artificial and alien surroundings, and still expect it to respond calmly, or cooly, or predictably.

We noticed that the harnesses were too stiff and too thin, and that they were cutting into the animals' skin. Sumian, Bernard, and Bonnici have therefore made very wide, nylon belts, which we hope the animals find more comfortable. It was not easy to put these new harnesses on Pepito and Chris-

Pepito has taught himself to climb the ladder leading to *Calypso*'s bridge

tobald, but, with the help of generous distributions of sardines, they were finally buckled into place, and we have begun our tests. There is a noticeable lack of enthusiasm on the part of the sea lions.

Three

At Liberty in the Sea

Calypso docked at Natal, on the coast of Brazil, late in the afternoon. A crowd of people was milling about on the pier, and as soon as they saw the two sea lions, there was a collective shout. Everyone pushed forward for a better look at the animals.

We had to move their cages in order to tie up, and while we were executing the final maneuvers of our docking operation, we were too busy to keep an eye on the cages. We were coiling our hawsers when Christian Bonnici noticed that Pepito was not only out of his cage but that half of his body was already off of the boat. He grabbed for the animal and succeeded in getting a grip on Pepito's hind legs. Pepito turned his head and bit down, hard, into Christian's stomach, keeping his jaws together for a full minute. Then, seeing that Bonnici would not release him, he opened his jaws and Bonnici quickly carried him over to his cage and locked him in. Since then, Pepito has been sulking, and he refuses to eat.

April 13. We noticed a new sound today, a sort of low moan, which the sea lions make while rubbing their snouts together.

At 10 P.M, we left Natal, but came to a halt almost as soon as we had left the harbor so that we could catch some fresh fish for Pepito and Christobald.

We lowered our lights into the water but nothing happened. The sea was rough, and there was a full moon. Our lamparo fishing was a complete fiasco.

April 14. Today is Easter Sunday. Pepito, in honor of the occasion, has decided to end his fast. This morning he ate mackerel.

We would like very much to be able to find some fresh fish for our sea lions. We've tried twice, once with hook and line and once more with the lamparo, but without catching a single fish. Is it possible that we are in an azoic area?

We noticed that Pepito was having trouble with large mackerel, so we have been removing the head and bones, as he watches, before handing him the fish. He swallows as many as seven of these large fish at one sitting.

Christobald, on the other hand, makes no such demands on us. Feeding him fish is like throwing them into a bottomless pit. If this keeps up, we are soon going to have supply problems.

April 15. The water around us has taken on a greenish hue, which indicates that we are approaching the mouth of the Amazon. We were surprised to find dolphins here, of a species whose tails are spotted.

April 16. This morning we moored off Cayenne. Our last freezer is empty, and it was absolutely necessary to find food for Pepito and Christobald. Bonnici and Sumian went ashore in search of a fishmarket. They found one which stocked frozen mackerel and bought out the entire stock. Unfortunately, it is mackerel imported from France by air, and the price was ridiculous. Still, Pepito and Christobald must eat.

Puerto Rico

A team headed by Falco has gone to St. Croix while *Calypso* is making for Puerto Rico.

Every day, Pepito and Christobald are making progress. They have now acquired the habit of making frequent visits to the wardroom, where they place their front paws on the table and upset the dishes. This seems to amuse them greatly.

Right above: Christobald, his whiskers at the ready, poises for a dive from *Calypso*'s aft deck

Right below: Pepito and Christobald dive with *Calypso*'s team for the first time. The sea lions are wearing harnesses and leashes

The equally frequent incursions into the passages has wreaked havoc with the good order and cleanliness of *Calypso,* since we have been unsuccessful in housebreaking either of the animals. We have tried everything, including a page taken from someone's experience in dealing with cats: a shallow container filled successively with sand, sawdust, ashes, and even algae. Nothing worked. Pepito and Christobald refuse to be turned into cats.

Even so, it is impossible to be angry with them. Christobald now sits happily on Michel Bernard's lap, and Pepito follows Raymond Coll like a dog, watching with obvious admiration everything that Raymond does, and listening as he speaks. Coll, who, as everyone knows, is not the most loquacious man aboard *Calypso,* engages in a continuous monologue when he is with Pepito. I do not know what he says, but Pepito seems to understand every word.

Pepito has turned into such an extrovert that sometimes we must scold him for being underfoot so much. On Seal Island, when we were trying every trick we know to capture a pair of the elusive sea lions, who would have believed that one of the animals would become so friendly in three months that he would actually be in our way?

May 9. Falco and his team have come by air to rejoin *Calypso* in San Juan, Puerto Rico.

One of our errands here is to find a larger pool for the sea lions so that we may have a full-scale rehearsal of our marine ballet with Pepito and Christobald before venturing into the open sea.

As luck would have it, we found a very kind lady who offered us the use of her magnificent pool. She had only one condition. She would have to participate in every phase of the work: in transporting Pepito and Christobald from *Calypso* to the pool, in the rehearsal, and in the filming itself. She was very candid about her reasons for this unusual request: "I simply adore sea lions."

Fortunately, we were in a position to take advantage of her adoration. We rented a station wagon and installed the sea lions in it. Then, with the lady, we set out, under the torrid sun, across Puerto Rico.

This was the sea lions' first automobile trip, and noise and the motion of the car made them nervous. Pepito insisted on climbing onto Yves Omer's lap, while Yves was driving. It was all Yves could do to bring the car to an abrupt halt on the shoulder of the road, as Falco and Sumian immobilized Pepito who was now trying to bite.

The lady, with a small shriek of fright, threw open the door and fled, leaving the door open behind her. A moment later, Christobald was strolling on the highway. Fortunately, he stopped, appearing a bit confused by the

AT LIBERTY IN THE SEA 67

strangeness of his surroundings. Sumian quickly seized him by the hind legs and carried him back to the station wagon.

The lady, meanwhile, had taken refuge in her own automobile, which her chauffeur had been driving along the road behind us.

By some chance, we had had the foresight to buy a large supply of squid at a San Juan supermarket before leaving. With the help of these delicacies, cut into pieces, we were able to make Pepito and Christobald do whatever we wanted. We waved a piece of squid before them like a carrot before a rabbit, and they settled back in the car. We waved another piece to make them leave the car, when we reached the lady's house, and to make them follow Falco through her garden toward the pool. There, the usefulness of the squid ceased. As soon as Pepito and Christobald caught sight of the water, they rushed forward and threw themselves into the pool with a great splash.

It was an ideal pool for our purposes, and the lady, who had forgotten her misadventure by then, was a perfect hostess to both sea lions and divers.

For four days — from May 12 to May 15 — Pepito and Christobald were subjected to a course of progressive training which gave us every hope that they would not escape once we transferred them to the open sea. They quickly learned to stay with their friends in the water, to remain by their side, to come at a simple signal. Teaching them such things would have involved many risks if we had attempted them in the sea.

For the first time since their capture, Pepito and Christobald had the run of a pool of sufficient size for them to enjoy. They also discovered that their friends, wearing diving equipment, were able to stay in the water as long as they, and that they were reasonably "at home" in that element — though not nearly so fast as the sea lions.

Falco was able to feed Pepito and Christobald at the bottom of the pool. He dived, then waited until they came to him, and offered them bits of squid. At this point, underwater taming was almost a reality.

On May 16, there was a new drama as we attempted to get Pepito and Christobald back to *Calypso* in our station wagon. Christobald — no one knows how — succeeded in getting half of his body through an open window. We had to slam on the brakes so as to stop before he fell onto the pavement, and Sumian grabbed the animal and shoved him onto Falco's lap, who held him motionless. This sent Christobald into a rage — or rather, into a tantrum, like a child. All the commotion made it impossible for Yves to drive properly, and there was an accident. Falco, Sumian, and the automobile were all covered with excrement, the automobile worst of all.

From that time to this, it has been impossible for anyone from *Calypso* to rent an automobile in Puerto Rico.

Pepito and Christobald no longer need their harnesses to make them remain with their friends

Left: The two sea lions are now free in the water

A refreshing dip with friends

On the Beach

The following morning, when everyone had recovered from their emotions of the previous day, we left the port of San Juan in search of a deserted beach where we could continue our experiment. Not far away, we found an empty bay bordered by a stretch of white sand. It seemed perfect for our purpose, and it was there that we decided to make our first dive with Pepito and Christobald.

It took the entire team to get the sea lions into the launches, one sitting on the bow of each boat. They were both wearing their harnesses and their leashes.

As we drew near to shore, Pepito and Christobald were in a state of high excitement. Coll was able to calm Pepito, but Christobald once more threw a tantrum. As soon as the launch had touched the beach, he fought free and jumped into the water. He fought like a lion, and it was impossible to restrain him with the leash. There was nothing to do but put him into a box and take him back to *Calypso.* I felt very sad and very sorry for Christobald. He had been unable to resist his instinct for freedom and the call of the sea. Yet, if he had escaped, encumbered as he was with harness and leash, and thousands of miles from his own island, he would have had no chance of survival. I have promised myself that one day we will set him free, but when we do, it will be in such a way that he may have a normal life.

As Falco watched Christobald returning to *Calypso,* he had a strong feeling that Christobald had not really tried to get away from us; that he had merely been overexcited by the proximity of the sea which he had seen every day of his life, but into which we did not allow him to venture. Bébert thinks that he can be trusted more than we believe.

Pepito presented no problems. He sniffed the water and trotted happily behind Raymond Coll on the beach, at the end of his leash. Raymond is immensely proud of him.

May 23. At dawn, *Calypso* was within view of the island of Tobago. We put the zodiacs into the water and set out in search of a creek for Pepito and Christobald's first dive. After inspecting several islands, we chose a rocky, deserted inlet, where the water was about fifty feet deep and where the bottom was covered with lovely coral — giant lavender sea fans and golden staghorn — and variegated fishes.

A team worked the entire morning to close off the mouth of the small inlet by means of a securely tied net, so as to minimize the chances of an escape.

By early afternoon, the net was in place. The divers' instructions for the moment were to allow Pepito and Christobald to become accustomed to the inlet. We would decide later whether it was safe to remove the net.

Once more, Pepito and Christobald were loaded onto the launches. Pepito, with Coll petting him constantly, was quite calm; but Christobald, for whom Falco was responsible, was excited and barked continually. Christobald is no doubt troublesome and overly excitable, but he has a vitality which I find extremely engaging. I could not help wondering, as I watched the animals, whether we were not expecting too much of them. After all, they had the right to demand their freedom, even by barking in a voice that threatened to shatter our eardrums.

We were counting on their affection and on their intelligence for them to accept us as friends, even once they had regained the security of their natural environment, the sea. Perhaps we had captured them too late in life. We would have had to take them very young for them to attach themselves to us as Konrad Lorenz' geese did to him. We had tried to make them love us, and we taught them never to fear us. Would that affection be sufficient to make them resist the lure of the open water?

Falco and Christobald climbed into the water. Falco was afraid that Christobald would strain at his leash and attempt to reach the open sea, but he did nothing of the kind. He remained at Falco's side every moment.

It was Pepito who, to everyone's surprise, circled the enclosed inlet, attempting to find a way out into the sea. Then he swam back to Raymond Coll, as though to ask him to point the way.

The sea lions cavorted around the divers and among the coral formations. They shot up toward the surface like rockets and then went spinning down toward the bottom, brushing against the divers with a twist of their bodies. Our marine cameras were eagerly filming the whole scene which, however, was somewhat spoiled by the presence of the sea lions' harnesses and leashes.

I gave the signal to end the exercise because I did not want an incident of any kind to compromise our first success.

After several days more of practice with the harnesses and leashes, I suggested that Falco and Coll continue the exercise without the restraints. I was convinced that the animals would continue to feel as though they were still wearing their harnesses and that that sensation would keep them near their companions. And I could only hope that they would not jump out of the enclosure.

Following page: An underwater ballet featuring Pepito and Christobald

The experiment was a success. Even Zoom seemed to understand that his web-footed cousins had now qualified for life without leashes — the same life which Zoom himself had led for so long with *Calypso's* men.

This phase lasted for several days. Then I decided that it was time for us to go on to the next stage, the success of which would depend above all on trust. We would find out whether the divers and the sea lions had established the kind of understanding which has existed for so long between man and dog.

We had planned to have the launches take Falco and Coll and the sea lions to a certain spot for their experimental dive in the open water. The two divers, however, thought it best not to use the launches. Instead, they took a supply of squid, and then simply invited Pepito and Christobald to follow them into the water from *Calypso*'s diving platform. They had looked forward a long time to this experience.

We had taken only one precaution, that of attaching a red float to the end of the sea lions' leashes. This would make it easier for us to find them if they attempted to escape. Other than that, they were completely free.

Falco and Coll dived to the bottom, about fifty feet below the surface, and waited. They saw the sea lions diving toward them in a cloud of bubbles, their whiskers alert. Obviously, they were looking for the two men. Then, a marine rodeo took place among the coral — a wonderful ballet during which Pepito and Christobald, whenever they came within reach of the divers, were petted and fed pieces of squid. Gradually, they were lured toward the enclosure where the first part of the experiment had taken place. Then I called a halt to the session.

The time had come to place our trust entirely in Pepito and Christobald. I felt instinctively that our entire program would be crowned with success on the day that Coll and Pepito, Falco and Christobald would be able to swim from *Calypso* to the enclosure without incident; that we would be ready for the final proof of trust when man and marine animal would both be free and inseparable in the open sea.

The nets blocking the entrance to the enclosure were brought back aboard *Calypso*. I asked the cameramen to check their equipment with special care, and I discussed with Michel Deloire the techniques of slow-motion filming and the positioning of the cameras in the water.

Our preparations were soon finished. The nets were on board, and the lookouts were in position in their boats. We were about to begin. I looked at the faces of the men around me and read emotions ranging from hope to worried uncertainty.

Pepito was the first one off the diving platform, followed closely by Coll.

Falco and Christobald dived together, a moment later.

The two sea lions reappeared on the surface almost immediately, as though trying to orient themselves. We have seen sea lions at the Cape do the same thing when they want to head for the open sea. Falco and Coll were no doubt waiting below the surface, hoping.

Then Pepito and Christobald disappeared again, and we knew that they had gone to join their companions on the bottom. It was undoubtedly the high point of the friendship between man and sea lion.

The return to *Calypso* was an extraordinary spectacle. Pepito and Christobald climbed the divers' ladder unaided; they were coming aboard in the same way that Raymond Coll and Albert Falco came aboard. Coll and Falco watched, smiling, as the two sea lions lifted themselves comically from rung to rung with their flippers. Pepito and Christobald, as though conscious of being admired, paused midway and gazed down at their two friends still in the water. They gave soft barks of affection and excitement.

This exceptional scene, denoting a perfect understanding between man and animal, finally dissipated the scruples I had experienced at Seal Island over making prisoners of our two friends.

I knew now that the presence of man among sea lions did not necessarily mean the death of the animals. We had proved that men and marine mammals are able to live together — as loyal and sincere friends — if only man is willing.

What was essential had now been done, and I was convinced that there was no longer any danger of escape. Pepito and Christobald had learned to trust us; now, we had to learn to trust them equally. After all, they were going to share our lives in the sea, to become our diving companions, and their attachment to us would undoubtedly increase as time went by.

What I wanted now was to see the two marine mammals not only accompany divers but also collaborate in their work beneath the surface. However, I wanted that collaboration to be free and spontaneous, on the part both of Pepito and Christobald and of the divers, so that the latter could have the sea lions with them only when they wished.

During this whole period, it was sometimes difficult to say what was work and what was play. I doubt, so far as Pepito and Christobald were concerned, that there was any difference. It was not quite the same thing for our divers. When they were working on the bottom, they were compelled to observe the various decompression stages in their ascent to the surface. But the sea lions shot up through the water like bullets, without showing the slightest trace of physical ill effects.

Pepito and Christobald had adopted our toboggan as a favorite play area. This was really a slide which we had installed on *Calypso*'s stern so as to enable several divers to enter the water in rapid succession. Once the sea lions had discovered that accessory, they never tired of sliding down into the water and then climbing out and sliding down again, over and over, like children at a playground.

At this time, we were at the Silver Bank, in the Caribbean, attempting to locate a sunken Spanish galleon which, it was said, contained a fortune in booty taken from the New World. The interest that this galleon held for us was somewhat less dramatic. The ship was covered by tons of coral, and our job was to dig it out.

For a long time, our search for the galleon was unsuccessful. Then, we happened upon the remains of an ancient ship* by discovering two cannon, half-buried in coral, which seemed to mark the location of the galleon we were looking for. This discovery was the beginning of a period of incredibly hard physical labor: digging out a ship encased in a tomb of limestone. As the days went by, our supplies of food and water grew short, and I decided that we would have to abandon our work, temporarily, so as to put into San Juan for supplies.

It also happened at this time that Bébert Falco had to return to France on another assignment, and I asked Serge Foulon to take charge of Christobald. En route back to the Silver Bank, near Mona Island, not far from Puerto Rico, Coll and Foulon took Pepito and Christobald for a swim. I watched as the two sea lions plunged joyfully into the water, never suspecting that it was there, near Mona Island, that Christobald would choose to return to the sea. But, beneath the surface, he parted company with Serge, who tried vainly to lure him back with pieces of squid. Our ship's captain, Roger Maritano, saw Christobald rise to the surface, turn to look at the small island, and then, deliberately, turn to the open water and begin to swim away. He noticed that the point at which Christobald appeared was a considerable distance from the divers' air bubbles, and he immediately gave the alarm.

It took time for Coll to return to *Calypso* with Pepito, to lock the animal in his cage, and to return to the launch with a net. By then, Christobald had a good headstart. But, since everyone was watching for him, he was sighted every time that he came to the surface to breathe.

The launch followed him for more than an hour, in very choppy water, as Michel Deloire filmed the dramatic chase. Once, the launch caught up to

*See *Diving for Sunken Treasure,* by Jacques-Yves Cousteau and Philippe Diolé, Doubleday & Co., Inc., Garden City, and Cassell, London, 1971.

The friendship between sea lions and divers was sealed among the corals and sponges of the Caribbean

Christobald, and Sumian, in the bow of the boat, even managed to touch him with the net. But Christobald was too familiar with nets. With a surprising burst of speed, he pulled away from the launch.

The boat's supply of gasoline was now almost exhausted, and Coll and his companions had to give up the chase, for *Calypso* was still moored off Mona Island, and Christobald was swimming in the opposite direction. Moreover, there was really little chance of recapturing him. Sea lions can swim at a speed of sixteen or seventeen miles per hour, and they are able to remain beneath the surface for twenty minutes at a time. It is believed that they are able to dive to depths of over 1,200 feet; and it is known that they are able to remain in the water almost indefinitely and even to sleep there, rocked by the waves.

The launch therefore returned to *Calypso* empty-handed, and to a disappointed, dejected group of men. Even Zoom seemed saddened. The next day, and on the days following, *Calypso* changed her position several times in order to allow the divers to continue their search, but there was no trace of Christobald, and we resigned ourselves to his disappearance. He had always been the more independent of the two sea lions, and the wilder; but his need for freedom was something that he shared with us, something that we could understand. I wished only that he had chosen a more suitable area for his escape. Long before, man had exterminated the hooded seals of the Caribbean; it hardly seemed the ideal place for a sea lion from the Cape of Good Hope to begin a new life.

I think that the one who took Christobald's escape most to heart was Pepito, who now wandered through *Calypso*'s passages like a lost soul, mourning the loss of his companion. Several times, he threw himself into Coll's arms in order to be consoled. His plight was truly touching.

Our fuel and water were now exhausted, and, with a heavy heart, we returned to Puerto Rico, some 250 miles away.

The first thing that greeted us in San Juan was a photograph of Christobald in a local paper, the San Juan *Star*. The picture showed a fisherman holding out a sardine to the sea lion. It seems that, in the nine days that Christobald was free, he had some difficulty in finding food. He swam at least a hundred nautical miles, from Mona Island to San Juan, then, probably famished, "surrendered" to the first man he met: a fisherman on a boat a mile out of port. The astonishing thing was that the fisherman did not spear Christobald, or strike at him with his paddle, but gave him a sardine and then slipped a rope around his neck. The fisherman's name was Juan Medina. I had never heard of him, but I suddenly conceived a great esteem for him.

A reporter from the *Star* visited *Calypso* Sunday night, but he seemed unwilling to part with whatever information he had. I therefore sent my wife, Simone, and Michel Deloire to find Juan Medina and, if possible, the people who, according to the story in the *Star*, had bought Christobald from the fisherman.

After an incredible visit to the Nautical Club, where the personnel there simply refused to disclose the name of the buyer, Simone and Michel somehow managed to solve the mystery. The buyer, they discovered, was a certain Mme. W., and Simone immediately telephoned her to arrange an appointment for me. The lady was not excessively cordial but she did agree to see me at six o'clock that evening.

Michel and I went together to see the lady. I had been forewarned that I would have to use "all my charm," and I was prepared to do so, at least to the extent that I have any "charm" at all.

Mme. W., her mother, and two children named Ricky and Randy greeted me graciously. I whipped out a copy of *The Living Sea* and inscribed it "To Ricky and Randy," then began talking about television shows and movies. I believe I even suggested that Mme. W. was perfect for a role in one of our productions.

The ice was now broken. Whiskey was served. It was agreed that Christobald would be returned to us.

The Return of the Prodigal

It was all arranged. We met the following day at the Yacht Club, and then went to Mme. W.'s villa to pick up Christobald. Raymond Coll was indignant because it turned out that the "pool" provided for Christobald was nothing more than a child's inflatable wading pool. Moreover, the space provided for the sea lion — a sort of dog run — was covered with excrement.

Before turning the animal over to us, Mme. W. wanted to prove that Christobald had developed a strong affection for her. "Look," she said. "See how much he loves me." She held out her hand to pet the sea lion. Christobald immediately sank his teeth into the hand, hard, and held on until we forced his jaws open. There were screams, and moans, and a simulated fainting fit.

Finally, the wound had been disinfected and bandaged, and we left in a convoy of five vehicles. In one, there was a reporter and a photographer from the San Juan *Star*. Eugène Lagorio and I were in the second car. In the third, John Soh, Michel Deloire, and Agostini were in the front seat, and Raymond Coll and Christobald in the back. Mme. W., her mother, and Ricky and Randy were in the fourth car. Bringing up the rear, in a truck, was the fisherman, Juan Medina, and a friend of his.

Traffic was heavy. Several times, the convoy was broken up, then re-formed. By the time we reached our destination forty-five minutes later, Christobald had had an attack of the colic, and Raymond Coll was covered with excrement from head to foot. The smell emanating from the vehicle was truly pestilential, and Agostini had been unable to restrain himself from vomiting out of the window of the car as it sped through San Juan.

At the end, there were pictures and television shots as Mme. W. fluttered about, cooing. Finally, at 6 P.M., there took place Christobald's triumphal return to *Calypso*. He and Pepito actually embraced.

A great feast had been arranged in honor of the prodigal's return. Even Zoom was in good spirits. Raymond, our chef, had prepared a banquet in the

Pepito and Christobald answer a summons by Raymond Coll

wardroom, and the main dish was squid *à la provençale*. Christobald, on this special occasion, ate at the table with us, though, it must be admitted, his manners left much to be desired.

The following morning, there was a long article in the *Star*, and a crowd of people touring *Calypso*.

It was with a sense of relief that we sailed out of the port of San Juan, on course for the Silver Bank, carrying supplies for two months.

One morning barely two weeks later, we awoke to find Christobald very ill. Foulon and many of the other men were convinced that his illness was an aftereffect of his Puerto Rican sojourn in the wading pool. And, in fact, Christobald had been very thin when he was returned to us.

As soon as we had him aboard *Calypso* again, we had put Christobald on a special diet. It seemed to work, but something had changed; Christobald was not as he had been before.

On the morning that he seemed so ill, Dr. Tassy was called for a consultation. He tried everything, even heart massage, but nothing seemed to do any good. By the next morning, Christobald was dead.

Feeding Pepito had now become a problem, since we had only a limited supply of food with us. We therefore tried to rely on local fishes. We began by feeding Pepito some pieces of grouper. The following morning, he was quite obviously ill. He vomited, and he kept his two hind legs over his stomach as though hoping to smooth away the pain. Everyone was thoroughly alarmed. No one mentioned Christobald, but it was easy to see that the memory of his brief agony was in everyone's mind. Dr. Tassy was called immediately, and he gave Coll a tube containing a suppository for Pepito, with instructions for its use.

The purgative worked magically. Two hours later — a period during which Raymond spoke to Pepito and massaged his stomach constantly — Pepito's bowels moved. Thirty minutes afterward, he was playing and diving in his pool.

Needless to say, we never fed Pepito grouper meat again. Instead, on certain nights of the week, after having spent the whole day hoisting great blocks of coral onto *Calypso*'s rear deck and breaking them open with sledge hammers, a team of volunteers fished from 10 P.M. to 3 A.M., to provide Pepito with a supply of a small fish — we called them needlefish — which he liked very much and which he had no trouble in digesting.

Finally, the lack of water, the exhaustion of everyone aboard *Calypso* — and, above all, the discovery that the ship we were working on was a hundred years younger than the ship we had been looking for — persuaded us to abandon our work at the Silver Bank. We had other work waiting for us in the Pacific.

The Panama Canal

For large ships, navigating the Panama Canal presents no serious problems. A team of specialists comes aboard and takes care of maneuvering the ship. *Calypso*, however, is too small to warrant such treatment, and she is too small for the locks to be filled specially for her. Therefore, whenever we pass through the Canal, we are coupled with a larger ship and we have to work the hawsers ourselves and also provide our own security measures.

Vessels do not move through the Canal under their own power, but are pulled by "mules" — small electric tractors running on rails. There are four mules assigned to each ship, two forward and two aft. By means of hawsers, the forward mules pull the ship, and the aft ones restrain it so that it will not crash into the gates of the locks. Here again, however, *Calypso* is underprivileged. She does not have a right to mules. Instead, she must be secured to a larger vessel by lines — "coupling," they call it — and she is pulled along vicariously, as it were, by the latter vessel's mules. There is some problem in this arrangement. For instance, there is a strong current when the lock is being filled, and one must be constantly on the alert against accidents.

Here are some entries from the log of Claude Caillart, who was *Calypso*'s captain when she passed through the Canal on this occasion:

"*Friday, September 20, 1968.* The pilot came aboard at eight o'clock and we started out immediately, secured by lines to a Cuban cargo vessel. We noticed that there was a detachment of U. S. Marines aboard the ship. I am told that this is a precaution taken only with Cuban ships in the Canal Zone.

"Lake Gatun is quite beautiful when seen from *Calypso.* The tops of trees rise up from the water — trees that were growing here before the Canal was dug. They are still alive, and their tops are like bright green bouquets floating on the surface of the lead-gray water.

"The entry into the Gatun lock is the most delicate maneuver of the entire passage through the Canal. A strong current fans out from the gate and tends to push the boat against the walls of the lock. But we were moving quite slowly, and with proper attention to our lines, we made it through the lock without incident.

"To port is a large tug, the *Rousseau,* which will take us from the first reach* to the second and third reaches. The water boils impressively as the locks are filled, and I must say that *Calypso* looked very small. . . .

"In the second reach, we drew alongside a freighter, the *Anjou.* We exchanged greetings by radio, and we have arranged to rendezvous at Callao, which is a regular port of call for the *Anjou.*

"The lock gate opened, and the Cuban cargo ship moved forward with *Calypso* following. We had to move rather quickly to come alongside her to starboard, and the chief pilot rushed up onto the bridge to register a complaint and to cite regulations. I explained why it had been necessary to move so quickly, and he left less angry than he had come.

"Even so, it was difficult to position ourselves properly with respect to the Cuban ship, and we were finally able to do so only by tacking at a level with the buoys and taking short cuts. The pilot still refuses to let us use the banana-boat canal, which is rather narrow but seems quite pleasant. The pilot is an interesting man. He wears a sun helmet, carries a briefcase, and is equipped

---

*The interval between the locks of a canal.

with a thermos of water.

"We slowed down at the entry to Gaillard Cut, the famous Culebra. There is an 848-foot tanker dead ahead. Moreover, the Canal is being widened in this section, from 300 to 500 feet. In a sudden squall, we took advantage of the delay to come alongside a Spanish merchantman just below the plaque commemorating the work of the French on the Canal.

"The big tanker had trouble entering the Pedro Miguel lock, despite the fact that it has four pilots aboard and is surrounded by four tugs. Finally, the mules took over. The gate closed, the chain across the gate tightened, and we had to put in next to the Canal wall to wait. It was a difficult operation because of a strong current astern, and *Calypso*'s hull moved constantly against a large rubber bumper.

"Finally, the tanker was out of the reach. The gate opened and we entered the lock without the help of the mules. We tied up by means of two lines forward and two aft. When we left the Pedro Miguel lock, we could see the tanker already in the Miraflores. The pilot signaled me to increase speed but this time, I was determined to observe the rules.

"It was even more difficult to put in next to the wall here than in the Pedro Miguel, since the current was stronger. Below, our hull was protected by a rubber bumper; above, however, the bumper is of wood, and *Calypso* shuddered as she moved against it. Also, her paint was scratched.

"The Miraflores lock has two reaches, and the passage from one to the other is made difficult by a strong current astern. We came up against one of the walls and tied up on an axis to it by tightening our hawsers.

"Finally, we entered the stretch in which the water level is the same as that of the Pacific. I was beginning to have my fill of canals and locks.

"As soon as the gate opened before us, we were caught in a downpour, complete with lightning and thunder. We moved from buoy to buoy, passing several freighters going in the opposite direction.

"Two vedette boats met us off Balboa, bringing our clearance papers, a supply of squid for Pepito, and a few loaves of bread for us.

"We passed under the Panama Bridge in heavy rain, and the pilot was put ashore at 6:30 P.M. — a worthy figure in his raincoat and sun helmet.

"We skirted the islands, then headed toward Palmelo."

I have decided to set Pepito free, as soon as I can do so in conditions that will make it possible for him to return safely to the wild. But it will have to be

Following page: The waters around Puerto Rico, where the sea lions and our divers swam together, are rich in marine life

in a place inhabited by other furred seals.

It would be useless to continue our experiment. We have already proved what we set out to prove: that marine mammals are almost as capable of attachment to humans as land mammals.

Moreover, the next project on our program will take us into the Andes, to Lake Titicaca, some 13,000 feet above sea level. We could leave Pepito aboard *Calypso,* I suppose; but there will be very few men aboard, and his presence and the surveillance that it entails will only add to the enormous amount of work that they have to do.

We are now en route from Callao to Mollendo, the Peruvian port from which we will begin the land journey to Lake Titicaca. I have asked Captain Caillart and everyone else to watch for one of the herds of sea lions which I know are quite plentiful along the Pacific coast of South America. I have an idea on how to go about releasing Pepito, and, in order to carry out the plan, I have invited two Peruvian specialists in marine mammals to visit *Calypso.*

September 30. At 8 A.M., we dropped anchor off the Chinchas Islands and sighted several sea lions on the beach. I sent out a launch with Raymond Coll in charge, since Raymond is fairly fluent in Spanish. On shore, he conferred with two representatives of the company which sells guano commercially, who informed him that they had just completed their collection.

Raymond reported that there were only a few sea lions on the island.

We raised anchor and made for the Ballistas Island farther south. We reached our destination at about noon and were visited by the caretaker, who came out to our anchorage in a rowboat and spoke at length to our two Peruvian experts.

Almost immediately, we sighted a group of sea lions napping in the sun on the beach. I sent out a launch with Canoë Kientzy, Jean-Paul Bassaget, and Dominique Sumian, to find out what species the animals belonged to. The men reported back initially that they had been unable to observe the sea lions closely, since as soon as they set foot on the beach all of them had rushed into the water. However, they found some excellent caves and estimated that there was a large number of sea lions on the island.

Their second attempt was more successful. They returned to *Calypso* with a sea lion about the size of Pepito. The new arrival was obviously unhappy and tried desperately to sink his teeth into his captors. We tried to put him into the net enclosure on the rear deck so that the Peruvians could examine him; but Pepito, usually so calm, suddenly became very excited, jumped over the enclosure, and dived into the sea.

Immediately, Maurice Leandri and Marius Barre set out in pursuit in the launch, equipped with a net and a supply of squid. But it was impossible to lure Pepito into the boat. He was willing to nibble at the squid, at arm's length, as he swam slowly toward land — then dived and disappeared. He seemed to bob up everywhere at the surface, but no one could tell if it was really Pepito or one of his cousins from the island.

Meanwhile, the Peruvian specialists had delivered their verdict. The sea lion from the island was of the species *Arctocephalus australis,* that is, the same species as Pepito. The only difference was that the local sea lion was more brown, and his nose was slightly longer.

I therefore contacted the launch by radio and told them to give up the chase and return to *Calypso.* I was even able to give a plausible reason: the anchor was dragging in the current, and Captain Caillart had to change his anchorage.

There was an air of slight tension aboard. Everyone suspected that I was up to something, and their fears were confirmed when I ordered the sea lion captured earlier to be put into the water. The animal swam away from *Calypso* and disappeared from view.

Then, everyone understood, and there was sadness aboard *Calypso* that day, on the bridge as well as on deck.

Still, it was the only solution. If we had kept Pepito with us any longer, he would have become irreversibly attached to us, and perhaps incapable of fending for himself in the sea.

When we undertake to intervene in an animal's life we assume a grave responsibility. I was conscious of it from the first moment, at Capetown. And, along with sadness, I experienced a sense of relief at having discharged that responsibility as best I could. The very fact that our sea lions and our divers shared their lives, however briefly, was an important step forward in the relationship between man and animal. Pepito and Christobald, even though they had both left us on different occasions, obviously had great affection for us. They have left us with this ineradicable memory: that, for more than a month, two marine animals were our willing companions in the sea.

That memory, however sweet it may be, cannot disguise the fact that our experiment was only partially successful. It is true that Pepito and Christobald, when they began diving without their harnesses and leashes, returned to *Calypso* of their own accord, and that they obeyed the orders of their adoptive fathers. Yet, we must admit that the bits of squid we fed them played a more important part in their behavior than their affection for us.

A final and rather ominous note closes the chapter on our experiences with Pepito and Christobald. I understand that a group of specialists, at San Diego, have picked up where we left off in our attempts to tame sea lions, and they have been more methodical and more successful than we were. How-

Calypso crosses one of the locks of the Panama Canal

ever, the sea lions are intended to be used for military purposes: to locate lost torpedoes. The U. S. Navy is already using another marine mammal — the pilot whale — to bring the torpedoes up to the surface.

PART TWO
Elephant Seal

Jean-Paul Bassaget, Bernard Chauvelin, and Jacques-Yves Cousteau aboard one of *Calypso*'s launches

Four

Hurricane at Guadalupe

The year 1968 was a period of unrelenting activity for all of *Calypso*'s men. Mission followed mission, and film followed film, often requiring the use of teams simultaneously in distant areas of South America and the Pacific.

The expedition proper worked at Lake Titicaca, exploring this unusually deep inland body of water by means of our one-man diving saucers, which we had transported across the Andes. At the same time, *Calypso* was cruising along the Pacific coast of North America, following the migration of the gray whales from the Arctic Ocean to Baja California.*

I was also scheduled to shoot a film on a marine mammal which has now become relatively rare, the elephant seal. We had occasionally encountered these animals during our expeditions, in the course of some of our calls at desert islands. The elephant seal is a giant amphibian, an enormous mass of flesh and fat. The impression it conveyed to us was one of shapelessness and irritability. But we had long been intrigued by the sounds they make, their mating habits, and above all by the long trunk-shaped nose from which they

*See *The Whale: Mighty Monarch of the Sea,* by Jacques-Yves Cousteau and Philippe Diolé. Doubleday& Co., Inc., Garden City, and Cassell, London, 1972.

take their popular name. (Their scientific name is *Mirounga mirounga*.) It is believed that their remote ancestors resembled dogs. Later, the species increased considerably in size and finally opted for the aquatic life. The elephant seal belongs to the order of Pinnipeds — which means simply that they have webbed feet.

Ted Walker, a friend of ours who is an expert on marine mammals, was with us aboard *Calypso* as we followed the gray whales from north to south, and we discovered that he is a passionate admirer of the elephant seal. He explained that when elephant seals venture onto dry land for their mating season, they become quite vulnerable. Every minute spent on land requires a great effort on the animal's part; in fact, because of the elephant seal's enormous bulk, it is barely able to move out of the water. It tires very quickly, and it suffers from the heat. Thus, when on land, it remains in a state of somnolence bordering on coma, and it awakens only to fight and to mate.

It is Ted's opinion that the elephant seal's lack of aptitude for life on land was responsible for its virtual disappearance during the nineteenth century. On land, it was impossible for it to escape human hunters, and for a century it was at the mercy of whalers who hunted it for its oil when whales were in short supply.

The whaler's method was to use boat hooks to herd the animals to the beach, where they beat them with heavy sticks. The elephant seals then dragged themselves into the water and saved the whalers the trouble of having to transport heavy cadavers or slabs of fat from land to their ships.

By 1880, the great herds of elephant seals of the North Pacific had been hunted so savagely that there remained no more than a hundred specimens which had taken refuge on the remote island of Guadalupe, 134 miles off Baja California.

Even after they came under the official protection of the Mexican Government, however, the elephant seals were not left in peace. They were saved from the hunters, but they were at the mercy of every curious zoologist and, worse, prey to teams which captured the animals to sell them to zoos.

This situation persisted until the species was in imminent danger of extinction. At that point, the Mexican Government intervened by stationing a permanent detachment of soldiers on Guadalupe to protect the elephant seals. There remained a sufficient number of specimens to multiply the species, but it was difficult to know the exact number since elephant seals are not easy to see, let alone to count: they are able to remain underwater for at least fifteen minutes, to dive to depths of a thousand feet, and to travel for over a mile beneath the surface. How can one take a census among such extraordinary creatures?

A female elephant seal preens herself

The fact is that, as vulnerable as elephant seals are while on land, they are practically invulnerable in the water, and they are superbly equipped for aquatic life. Unlike whales which have only a single horizontal tail, elephant seals are equipped with two rear limbs modified into vertical flippers. These flippers move laterally, like the tail of a fish, and the forward flippers make it possible for the elephant seal to maneuver with a grace and ease that is surprising in so massive an animal.

None of us had been able to spend enough time among elephant seals to study their living habits and to discover whether or not, behind their forbidding exteriors, they were truly endowed with that originality which I sensed in them.

Guadalupe has remained the main gathering place of elephant seals during the mating season, and I decided to send a reconnaissance team to the island. It had to be done immediately, for these mammals come on land only to mate, and, in the case of the females, to bear their young. Beginning in March or April, they would return to the water and remain there for at least seven months, for elephant seals are nomadic creatures, and they spend more than half the year roaming the seas without coming on shore to rest.

Mounting an Expedition

One of our teams, which was aboard the *Polaris* — a boat we had rented — had already encountered elephant seals in the Pacific. Very bad weather had forced them ashore on a small island, a few hours out of San Diego, named San Benito. They had been astonished to come face to face with these great masses of flesh, roaring, staring at them, and moving their heads in the style of boxers at the beginning of a match. The animals were not very handsome, our men admitted, but they could not help admiring the courage with which they stood up to the intruders who were determined to take their pictures.

Our team's account of the elephant seals intrigued me deeply but it was not to San Benito that I wanted to go. It was to Guadalupe, where the elephant seals are totally protected by Mexican law and where, it seemed to me, we could find the largest number of them. My general plan was to put a team ashore to live among the elephant seals for a period of time and to get as much footage as possible of the animals, both on land and in the water.

It required only two days to organize the expedition. My son Philippe was in charge of all phases of the work, including obtaining the necessary authorization from the government of Mexico, purchasing the necessary camping equipment and the various accessories that would be needed — ranging from a handful of large nails to a hurricane lamp. They would also need a generator, an air compressor (to refill the divers' air tanks), marine cameras and land cameras, photographic equipment, and tape recorders.

One major logistical problem was water. Guadalupe is simply a rock in the ocean. It has no resources of any kind, not even fresh water. Philippe solved the problem by buying an impressive number of plastic jerry cans. He also had the ingenious idea of taking along some live chickens which a poultry farmer had guaranteed were good layers. Naturally, some chicken wire had to be included among the essential supplies, for a chicken coop. (Unfortunately for the chickens, they proved to be bad sailors, and they were so upset by the voyage that they were able to produce only an occasional egg. Their fate was that of all bad layers: they ended up in the pot.)

Finally, all the supplies, including a zodiac, tanks of compressed air and of fuel, and a frying pan (which was a last-minute acquisition) were loaded onto a small boat, the *Searcher,* which was supposed to transport men, supplies, and chickens across 120 miles of sea, from San Diego to Guadalupe, in one night.

Setting Up Camp

To everyone's surprise, it did so. In the morning light, the island appeared, high, hostile, and huge. The sea was choppy; the sky, a mass of gray clouds moving swiftly from east to west. Everyone was shivering with cold and everyone felt somehow inadequate before the steep rocks, the thundering breakers, and the magnitude of the task before them.

The first chore was to unload the material onto the beach, and everyone was astonished at the amount of equipment that, in San Diego, had seemed absolutely necessary. The *Searcher* dropped anchor before a shingle beach, above which towered a rock-covered mountain sprinkled with thickets. Far above, the men could see a few trees protruding through the fog.

The shore of the island was dotted with the huge, black, recumbent forms of elephant seals. Occasionally, one of the animals rose and dragged itself a few feet over the beach. From these forms rose hair-raising screams, mysterious sounds, and, above all, an unbearable stench.

The men from the *Searcher* were so busy unloading that they barely had time to do more than glance at the elephant seals. At first, they were deafened by the noises of the animals, but they quickly became accustomed to them, as one accustoms oneself to the din of a factory. So far as the smell was con-

Male elephant seals have a strange, fleshy growth above their trunks

A crowded beach at Guadalupe

Our landing party takes over the dilapidated buildings formerly occupied by a detachment of Mexican soldiers

cerned, it was all the men could do to keep from vomiting. But this, too, passed; as do all human trials.

Thanks to a pulley rigged up between the boat and the beach, the job of unloading was carried out in short order, and soon a hundred square yards of beach were littered with boxes, bags, jerry cans, and sundry items of equipment. The elephant seals nearby seemed hardly to notice this invasion of their sanctuary. There were many hundreds of them, perhaps more than a thousand. They lay there, apathetic, but lying in tight rows and apparently determined not to make way for the intruders. They stared at the men through large, round, brown eyes — myopic and dreamy eyes which also betrayed perhaps only the vaguest hint of irritation. But there was no trace of fear.

Philippe and his men, in order to make room for themselves, had to push the animals a bit. Then, the elephant seals moved, rising to the accompaniment of groans, lifting their heads and dragging themselves aside resentfully. Occasionally, one of the animals — a particularly large one — simulated an attack, but it was done without enthusiasm.

Guadalupe seemed to have been abandoned by humans, though there were still the ruins of the houses which, fifty years earlier, had been occupied

Females are more approachable than males

Left: Bernard Delemotte, after much patient effort and diplomacy, succeeds in petting an old male's trunk

by the Mexican soldiers assigned to protect the elephant seals. Our team decided to make use of these ruins, and they gathered up their material, which was still stacked on the beach 150 feet away, and carried it to the buildings. This chore was carried out in silence and took two hours. By nightfall, the ruins were fit for use. The roofs had been repaired, and several of the buildings had been cleared so as to serve as storehouses and depots. The tent had been pitched, and the kitchen set up in a convenient corner. An ancient shed, which seemed relatively impervious to the weather, was designated as a storage area for our cinematographic equipment.

The area was not an unattractive one. Thickets grew in the midst of the ruined buildings, and the buildings themselves, though dilapidated, were not desolate. They had managed to retain a peculiar charm — that of a Mexican village which has been reclaimed by nature. Red and purple mountains surrounded the camp on three sides, and the north shore was always crowned by clouds. The birds were so bold that they pecked for food at the very feet of the men; and the cats of Guadalupe, abandoned there by the Mexicans, quickly adopted the men of the expedition. It is possible that they had designs on the chickens, but these were kept securely locked in their coop.

Stormy Weather

There was still much to do the following day before contact could be established with the elephant seals and before shooting could begin. The arduous nature of the work was aggravated by the fact that there were relatively few men to do it. The compressor had to be installed, the tanks and cameras loaded, wood collected for the stove, and so forth. As these tasks were being performed, it was noted that the sun only occasionally shone through the clouds, and the water was becoming increasingly rough. Obviously, it would not be possible to do any shooting.

When the work was finished, therefore, Philippe and his men decided to explore the island around their camp. Guadalupe is a volcanic island of black rock which rose out of the sea only seven million years ago. It is rimmed with shingle beaches covered with rocks of unequal size. These rocks are the favored napping places of the elephant seals.

One of the first things that the divers found was a large pot, once used to melt fat. It was a relic of the whalers who had hunted the elephant seals for their oil. (Some elephant seals have a layer of fat four inches thick.) There was a vivid contrast between this reminder of the days when this beach was the scene of a massacre and the present time when the elephant seals, lords of all they survey, sleep peacefully on their rocks.

Access to the beach was full of snares. To climb over rocks carrying a camera tripod requires sure footing and steady nerves. At the beginning of their stay on Guadalupe, it took a half-hour for the team to go from their camp to the water; by the end, it required only fifteen minutes. If one of the men had fallen and injured himself on the rocks — it would have been easy to break a leg — it would have been impossible to get medical aid for him until the return of the *Searcher*.

Every day the men mingled with the animals. It was not difficult for them to do because elephant seals sleep most of the time. But, when they awaken, it is always in panic. They rise, their trunks raised threateningly, and roar. This,

On the raised head of a male, one can distinguish the two large nostrils at the extremity of the trunk, and, below, the mouth surrounded by whiskers

Following page: The male elephant seal is a peevish animal. When it is cross, it raises its trunks and emits a resounding roar

however, is a tactic of intimidation. Whenever it happened, Philippe responded by screaming as loudly as the elephant seal, and it was the elephant seal who was intimidated and backed off.

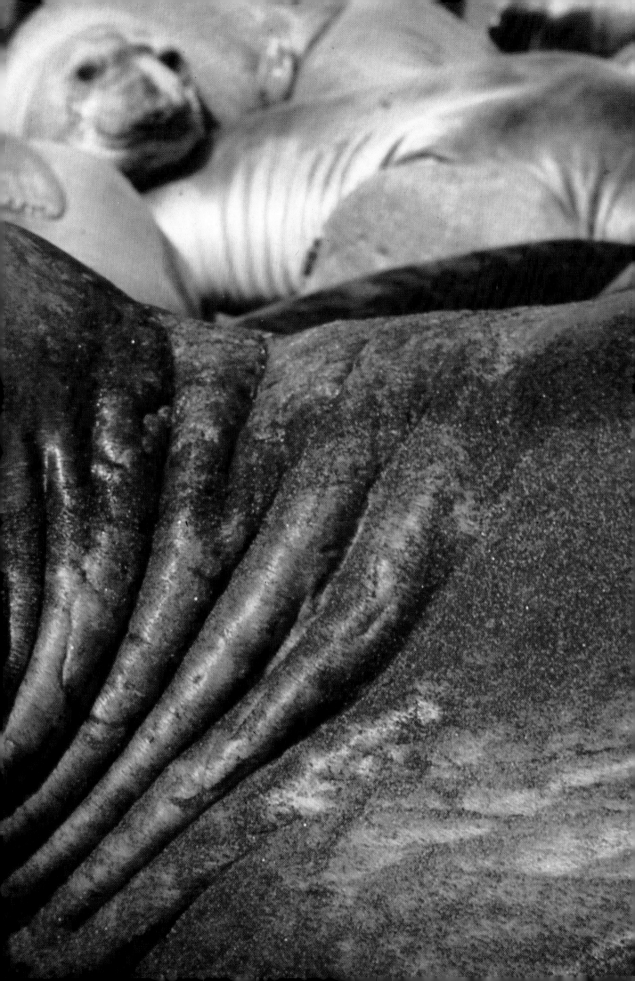

Usually, the cameramen took advantage of the animals' torpor to shoot scenes in silence: young elephant seals yawning, scratching themselves with their flippers, sneezing, or turning around to see what was going on behind them. The latter maneuver is accomplished by the animal twisting its neck until it is almost doubled over itself. It is a graceful movement and, if one waits long enough, there is always a young elephant seal who performs it.

Even after a week on Guadalupe, it was not easy for our men to predict the reactions of the animals. The basic rule they followed was never do anything that the elephant seals might interpret as a challenge.

Bernard Mestre and Serge Foulon had an idea for a new method of approach. Instead of moving toward the animals upright or on their knees, as they had done until then, they imitated the elephants themselves and approached them in a crawl, wearing their black diving suits. It proved to be an excellent tactic. A man crawling frightened the animals less than one walking upright.

It appears that, from the elephant seal's point of view, anything vertical is hostile. It seems hardly likely that the present generation of animals has learned to be wary of humans, despite man's record of slaughter. The explanation is probably that an upright form represents another male, and a challenge. On the other hand, any recumbent form represents a female. In order to make friends with an elephant seal, therefore, the thing to do is to drag oneself over the rocks. It is not always comfortable, but it is effective. Serge, following this method, was able to lie down against a great-trunked male without eliciting the slightest reaction from the animal.

Despite this increasing familiarity, no one of the team ever succeeded in distinguishing one elephant seal from another. There were so many of them, and they were so shapeless, that they sometimes looked more like large bags abandoned on the beach than marine mammals.

Diving

In the sea, the elephants usually remained just at the edge of the beach, moving back and forth in the swell, sliding on the foam-covered rocks, and swimming in the shallow water. This made it quite hazardous for the divers to observe the animals in the water, for the breakers were quite violent and certainly capable of dashing a man against the rocks, or even against a possibly short-tempered elephant seal. For, in the water, the animals' attitude toward man was the opposite of what it was on land. Here, they seemed to fear man, and they fled as soon as they saw one of the divers. It may be that

Young females, even in the water, have a gentle look about them

they confused our men with their great natural enemies, sharks and killer whales. Certainly, they took our team for a group of dangerous marine animals of some kind.

There were places specially favored by the elephant seals, such as shallow pools surrounded by rocks. If one surprised them there, it was possible to block the only exit through the rocks and film them in their hideaway. When our cameramen did so, however, the elephant seals panicked immediately, or went into a rage, and charged. On one occasion, the visor on Philippe's marine camera was crushed; and several times the cameramen had to beat a hasty retreat before the elephant seals.

In the course of one of these encounters, Bernard Delemotte was bitten by a young elephant seal; but, fortunately, Bernard was wearing his diving suit at the time, and the animal's teeth did not break the skin.

There were also long periods of playing hide-and-seek with the elephants in clouds of bubbles and foam and among hard rocks. These sessions always ended in the same way, with the divers lying exhausted and breathless in the bottom of the zodiac after a long and unsuccessful chase.

The marine vegetation around the island was exceptionally abundant. A growth of thick, fleshy algae covered the rocks and the bottom. The water was warm — 60°F — and there were many fishes, the most remarkable of which were the Garibaldi, which are colored a brilliant scarlet.

Our divers had sufficient leisure to observe the flora and fauna, since it was almost impossible for them to approach the elephant seals in deep water. At the slightest provocation, the animals herded together in tight ranks and if the divers moved toward them, they were greeted with open, menacing mouths. But in the water, at least, the men were not subjected to the deafening roars of protest which, on land, were amplified by the echo against the black cliffs.

The divers tried swimming among the long brown algae and taking hold of the fins of the more peaceful elephants; but even these, with a twist of their backs, shot away immediately. The elephant seal is as graceful in the water as it is clumsy on land. It is a very fast swimmer and is able to turn, stop, or change direction with astonishing speed. Its massive body, once in the water, becomes fluid and enormously mobile, and its eyes take on a reddish cast — probably due to the refraction of light.

Contrary to popular belief, the two-pronged appendage visible behind the elephant seal's body is not its tail, but its hind legs, which are webbed. The tail, which is very short, is located between these two hind legs.

Elephant Seal Harems

The team dived every day at Guadalupe, despite the unfavorable weather and the rough sea. The divers never gave in to the temptation to let down their guard in the water, for an elephant seal's bite can be a serious wound. The larger animals exhibit two long canine teeth, of which they make effective use when they fight among themselves. These seemed particularly dangerous.

An intriguing aspect of our men's stay at Guadalupe is that of the elephant seal's reaction to the divers. It was evidently one of surprise, for the animals often gathered to observe them. Yet, they were careful to keep their distance. In the water, their behavior resembled not at all that of Pepito and Christobald, and they were not playful. Rather, they were serious, distant, and vaguely hostile.

As the days went by, Philippe and his friends learned to respect these formidable animals and to esteem them for their courage. Even the smallest of them would attack if it felt threatened.

Life on the island was not without its charm. It was a tranquil place, and the elephant seals offered the opportunity for a fascinating study in a solitude favorable to work. This solitude was broken only by the friendly visits of

Elephant seals are much more agile in the water than on land, and it is difficult to foresee what the reactions of this mountain of flesh will be in the sea

members of the Mexican coast guard, who came with offers of help and gifts of fresh goat meat from animals hunted on the island.

At five o'clock one morning, Bernard Delemotte and Philippe scaled a cliff which separated their camp from a neighboring beach. Below them, on the rocks, they saw approximately two hundred elephants. All the females were gathered together into a tight mass of compact, groaning flesh, while a male promenaded around them. Apparently, no female was allowed to leave the group while the male was in attendance. If another male approached, the first animal raised its trunk, gave a terrible roar, and charged the intruder.

Seen from the height of the cliff, the beach was divided into distinct sectors. To the left, there were a number of calves and immature animals, probably born during the preceding year. In the middle was a group of females with the largest male of the herd. To the right, there was a less numerous harem of four or five females with a smaller male.

At 8 A.M., the large male crawled down to the water, as the females slowly followed. This patriarch was over fifteen feet in length. (There are specimens twenty-two feet long.) His trunk was also sizable — about two feet in length.

The females remained near shore, playing in the waves, until the male disappeared. Finally, the other elephants on the beach, except for the calves, crawled into the water and allowed themselves to be rocked in the undertow.

A Rodeo

A careful approach, caresses, the offer of live fish — nothing seemed to work. Philippe was therefore determined to try something else. He had read that if one immobilizes the trunk of an elephant seal, the animal immediately becomes docile. It seemed worth the attempt, and Philippe selected, as his subject, a male of medium size.

Bernard Delemotte chose, for a lasso, a thick rope which would not hurt the animal; and Serge Foulon got into the water so as to be able to approach the victim as it returned to the beach. The rest of the men lined up along the water, so as to miss nothing of what was going to happen.

As the male approached, it caught sight of Serge crawling on the rocks, and charged, roaring ferociously, its war cry echoing among the rock walls of the fault which opens onto the beach, its bulk pushing aside the rocks in its path. It resembled nothing so much as an outraged locomotive.

For a moment, the other men were afraid for Serge. He seemed so small, and the elephant seal, so large. Everyone had seen this particular male, with one stroke of its teeth, cut a piece of wood the size of three baseball bats. . . . Its weight alone would have been enough to crush a man bigger than Serge.

But Serge was planning to make use of the animal's clumsiness and, thanks to his own agility, he was never in real danger. With the skill of a true cowboy, he swung his lasso and caught the elephant's trunk on the first attempt. At that point, the battle began. The elephant seal had not read Philippe's book. Instead of becoming docile, it went wild and charged toward Serge with renewed vigor. Then, suddenly, it changed its tactics, turned, and began moving back toward the water, dragging behind him Serge, as well as Bernard Delemotte who had hold of the rope.

Amid uproarious laughter, the two marine cowboys returned to the beach, defeated, exhausted, and altogether deprived of confidence in the printed word.

The following morning, the male was back on the beach, calmly surveying his harem as though nothing had happened.

A Heroine

Guadalupe is inhabited by goats descended from those which were long ago abandoned by whalers or pirates. They were a constant temptation to men who, although sworn enemies of useless slaughter, were hungry for fresh meat. It did not seem wrong to select a victim from the herd of wild animals which, after all, had ravaged the island's vegetation. Moreover, the sailors from the Mexican coast guard would probably kill the goats anyhow. . . .

On the basis of such logic, two of the divers — those most gifted as mountain climbers — left at dawn. They returned during the afternoon, at the end of their strength, explaining that the goats were incredible acrobats, completely unapproachable, and unbelievably smart. Nonetheless, they had managed to kill one, which was immediately skinned, cooked, and eaten.

This particular goat, it transpired, had left the herd in order to cover its flight and had attacked the hunters singlehandedly.

A Nightmare

In the first days of March, when the mission on Guadalupe was drawing to a close, there was a sudden increase in the velocity of the wind. By evening, there was every sign of an impending storm. But the team was exhausted, and, after tying down everything that might be blown away, the men turned in for the night.

By three o'clock in the morning, the gusts of wind were so strong that one of the tent pegs gave way. A few moments later, the rest of them were gone. The tent collapsed onto the sleeping men, sending down lamps and clothing on their heads. Everyone was out of their sleeping bags as quickly as they could be, and their first effort was in holding down the tent which seemed in imminent danger of blowing away. The rest of the night was spent in devising various methods, all unsuccessful, of making the tent stand.

Meanwhile, the roofs of the old houses, which were nothing more than rusted sheets of tin, blew away one after the other, exposing our precious equipment to the storm. More easily replaced items, such as pots and pans, scurried across the ground as though endowed with life, always staying several feet ahead of anyone who attempted to catch them. There was only one

Following page: This male is lord of a harem, and he is on his way to join his wives

advantage to the storm: it drove away the mosquitoes which, from the first day, had plagued the team.

In the light of dawn, the damage seemed irreparable. Everything had been blown about. The rocks were littered with pieces of cloth and equipment and diving suits. The sheets of tin from the roofs were everywhere. The entire camp would have to be rebuilt. But the wind was still blowing and when the men tried to carry the tin roofs back to the houses, the gale ripped them from their hands and scattered them around as before. Even the food was ruined, spoiled by the rain or by the sea.

It was not until noon that the wind slackened a bit and the *Searcher,* which had brought the team to Guadalupe, appeared in the bay. Fearing the worst, it had come looking for survivors. However, it was impossible to land because of the rough sea, and a shouted conversation took place between the boat and the beach. Without knowing it, the occupants of the boat succeeded in restoring the courage of the men on land. Not because of anything they said, but because they seemed in even worse condition than our team on shore. It had not been a pleasant journey to Guadalupe through the storm.

By evening, when the *Searcher* disappeared over the horizon, the five men on land had virtually restored order to their camp.

An Understanding

Good weather came quickly. The last few days on the island were magnificent, and Philippe was able to get some very good underwater footage.

The elephant seals by then were becoming accustomed to the presence of humans and no longer seemed to notice their comings and goings. This provided an excellent opportunity to observe the animals at close quarters. Philippe and his friends discovered that the animals were much more "emotional" than they had first thought. They exhibited anger and violence, but they were also playful, and they demonstrated a capacity for tenderness. And, whereas in the beginning all elephant seals had been alike, now the divers were convinced that they differed, if not in appearance then at least in personality. This was especially true of calves between two and four months old. They were three or four feet in length, quite fat, short-necked, and covered with very soft fur which, when dry, was a lovely silver gray. With their round eyes, always on the verge of tears, they resembled "the kid" in the old Charlie Chaplin films.

The females were more approachable than the males, and, at the end of their stay, the divers sometimes napped with the backs of females as their

This harem of females on the beach is at the complete disposal of its master

pillows. On such occasions, other elephants usually came to lie down next to the divers for their own naps.

Serge Foulon seemed especially capable of winning the confidence of the animals, and he spent hours petting and playing with the young ones and rolling them in the sand — a game which they particularly enjoyed.

It was almost with regret that our first team on Guadalupe Island saw the *Searcher* arrive to take them back to San Diego. But it could not be helped. Water was becoming scare, food supplies were exhausted, and no one had the courage to suggest another goat hunt. Yet, there was almost a melancholic air as Philippe and the others loaded their equipment onto the *Searcher,* climbed into the boat, and watched the high black cliffs of the island disappear into the fog.

Their final report was sufficiently encouraging for me to decide on a sixty-minute sequence on elephant seals, to be shot on Guadalupe. I immediately began preparations for the expedition. There were supplies to be purchased, personnel to be organized — the thousand details that must be attended to before each of *Calypso*'s cruises no matter of how short duration that cruise will be. And, of course, there is research to be done. We always try to amass all available information on the subjects of a projected film. This not only saves time in our work, but also enables us to take advantage of the observations of divers and scientists who have preceded us in the field. In the sea as elsewhere, no one — regardless of his experience and expertise — works independently of the rest of mankind. *Calypso*'s men build on the work of others, as we hope that those who come after us will build on our work.

Five

A Question of Territory

The reconnaissance of Guadalupe Island and the first contact with elephant seals undertaken by Philippe and his friends were the preliminaries to a project which was to occupy our attention during the winter. The film brought back by the team seemed very promising, and I had decided to mount a full-scale operation at Guadalupe. A message was dispatched to *Calypso*, which was then off the coast of Peru. She proceeded northward along the Pacific coast of the American continent to Long Beach, California, and, after taking on supplies, made for Guadalupe.

Captain Claude Caillart's log describes *Calypso*'s arrival:

"*Friday, December 27, 1968.*

"We dropped anchor on the north side of the island, off the beach where Philippe and his team had landed in March. Philippe, Canoë, Michel Deloire, and Yves Omer went ashore in a zodiac and immediately established contact with the elephant seals, who shuffled around a bit but seemed rather passive.

"*Calypso* then skirted the eastern coast of the island, on the lookout for more elephant seals and for seals. There were elephants on the rocky beaches — they became fewer as we proceeded southward — and also sea lions on the rocks.

A male elephant
seal roars a
challenge to
another male

"At 1:15 P.M., we anchored off our southern point of disembarkation. A launch took Jean-Paul Bassaget ashore and returned carrying three foot soldiers of the Mexican marines. We offered them drinks, and they left with gifts and in the best of spirits.

"We weighed anchor at 3 P.M and headed toward our anchorage on the north side of the island. . . . We dropped anchor initially in 18 fathoms of water, but we were too close to shore, and I decided to change our position. We moved to 35 fathoms. The bottom is somewhat sloping here, but it is the best we can do for the present.

"It is 5:30 P.M., and it is already dark. Captain Cousteau has instructed us to set our watches back one hour at midnight.

"Philippe returned to *Calypso* to make his report. He was not able to shoot any unusual footage, but he did bring back a billy goat on the hoof. Morgan, our chef, was indignant, and the goat was taken back to the island and turned loose.

"We are going to begin work at 5:30 A.M. tomorrow. At 2:45, Captain Cousteau was awakened by the male elephant seals fighting on the beach.

"*Saturday, December 28.* Our camera team went ashore at 6:20 and waited on the beach for the sun to rise, intending to film some of the encounters between the males, and also the young ones nursing. Most important,

The challenged male
responds

they are going to try to get some footage of a female giving birth — which I am told will be very difficult.

"A diving saucer was prepared, then another team, composed of Omer, Sumian, Canoë, and Pierre Gauret, left with a zodiac to get some underwater footage near the coast.

"The elephant seals are not very fearful. They stay in shallow water, letting themselves drift in the swell, and it is rather risky to go near them. Sumian was bitten on the arm, but it was not a serious wound.

"I went ashore later and, after slipping on a rock, I tried to herd the elephants toward the divers. They are very difficult to move.

"The diving saucer went down but discovered nothing unusual.

"Captain Cousteau decided that the cameramen and a watch detail should spend the night on the beach in the hope that they would spot an elephant seal giving birth. However, no one saw anything. All of the females spent the night gathered into heaps, probably to hide the one which was giving birth.

"The weather is dreary. It drizzled all morning, and in the afternoon it began to rain in earnest.

"Bernard and Jean-Clair Riant reported in triumph that they've sighted a female in labor. The cameramen hurried to the spot, but it was all wasted effort. They returned to *Calypso* at 3:30 P.M., discouraged and drenched. At 7 P.M., they went ashore for another night on the beach."

Overly Modest Females

As Captain Caillart's log mentioned, I had hoped that we would be able to get some footage of a female giving birth during our first few days on Guadalupe. This would have enabled us to establish an over-all plan for the film by giving us a "slant." What I had not taken into account was the surprising modesty of the elephant seals. We did everything that we could think of, but we were unable even to get a glimpse of such an event. I think that the female elephant seals, like many wild mammals, give birth only when the circumstances are just right, and especially under cover of darkness.

Caillart's log continues:

"*Monday, December 30.* I accompanied the teams going ashore this morning, and I was assigned the job of using my binoculars to watch for a female in labor. I saw nothing.

"Michel Deloire has gotten some excellent mating footages; and Philippe has filmed a long and very bloody battle between two males.

"We've seen a number of battle-scarred males — some of them with their trunks half torn off.

"The divers are continuing to explore the deep-water areas, and the elephant seals appear to be getting used to them. Omer witnessed a mating in the water. He also saw something — a shark perhaps, or a killer whale — diving vertically."

The Battles

As soon as we arrived at Guadalupe, I was struck by the great number of elephant seals on the island. The beaches were literally black with them. Philippe assured us that they were much more numerous then they had been in the previous year. On land, there was an impression of bodies stacked everywhere and of disorder bordering on pandemonium. The giant males, in going down to the water, trample screaming baby elephants. Sometimes, even after that living steam roller has passed over them, the calves appear unhurt. They are still very flexible and soft — almost elastic. But many of them die. The males do not even bother to look at the calves.

It may be that they have other things on their minds. These great mammals cannot be comfortable in their present situation. The time was when *Mirounga mirounga* was found over a much larger area than now, along the Pacific coast from the Aleutians to the Canal Zone. Now, most of that area is closed to them because of human civilization. Elephant seals spend over half the year in the water, but once a year they must return to land in order to mate and rear their young. So, while their numbers increase because they are protected by law, the elephant seals have only one place remaining where they may take refuge during the mating season: Guadalupe, which has become their exclusive preserve.

By a curious paradox, the fact that the species is so wild is responsible for their situation. The great number of them presently occupying the relatively small area of the Guadalupe beaches is compromising their biological equilibrium, their social life, and perhaps their mental equilibrium as well.

We cannot manipulate the existence of animals with impunity — nearly exterminate them, then allow them to increase — without simultaneously upsetting the rules of life, the ecological conditions which the species itself has developed over thousands of years. The species most sensitive to such interference are the animals who live in groups, such as the elephant seal — and man.

In earlier days, the social structure of the elephant seals was clearly defined. The male reigned over a harem of a dozen females, which was confined to a determined area of the beach. This area was the territory of the male, and he defended it ferociously.

The species constituted a hierarchical society, in which the distinctions were visible to zoologists who were dealing with fewer animals scattered over a larger area. Today, how can one distinguish social structures in a species the individuals of which are literally piled into one small area? The laws governing the colony must necessarily have been changed by the increase in population density.

It follows that the logical, necessary defense of a male elephant seal's territory is no longer possible. All of the animals — males, females, and calves — are mingled indiscriminately. Occasionally, a male will still issue a challenge at large, and the challenge is accepted by any male who happens to be in the mood for an encounter. The challenge and its acceptance now have little to do with territory. The adversaries stand erect to meet, bracing themselves on their rears and executing some unbelievable contortions. Sometimes they draw themselves up vertically so as to be able to let their entire weight fall on their adversary. There is still an aggressive sense among the elephant seals, but that sense no longer has meaning. They meet in combat not to defend a territory, but to keep or to acquire a female, or merely to find an

Two males of about equal size meet in combat, chest to chest. Each of them tries to grasp the trunk of the other between its teeth. Both animals are wounded in the neck and their blood drips into the sea

outlet for their tendency toward violence and to satisfy a bellicosity which has lost its reason for being. For they exist in a society where all territories are confused and overlapping and where the social hierarchy is inoperative.

There is another striking characteristic of the elephant seals which others may or may not have noted: the calves seem to belong to no one in particular.

As soon as they are born, they want to nurse; but often the mothers, who appear indifferent to their young, have already returned to the water, leaving their babies unattended on the beach. The calf then crawls around until it finds an unoccupied teat. Thus, at Guadalupe there is a sort of milk bank and sex bank on the beach, where females accept any male or nurse any baby that happens along. Some calves are unable to find adoptive mothers, and they wander around the beach, pushing their noses into every stomach, crying from hunger. These orphan calves are often crushed by the heedless adults. Infant mortality appears to be astonishingly high.

One can get an idea of the population density of the elephant seals at Guadalupe when one approaches the beach from the open sea. The island is quite high, and the animals are all assembled at sea level, at the foot of the cliffs. Their noises are amplified by the walls of rock and sent out over the water. The effect, from the water, is bizarre; the sounds are those of a mob gone mad.

We discovered another gathering of elephant seals on the northern coast of the island, where the animals are even more numerous than on the beach facing *Calypso*'s anchorage. Here, too, as might be expected, the noise is deafening. Each of the sounds no doubt has a special meaning, and all together they constitute a complex of sounds, expressing calls, cries of hate, challenges, and so forth. I asked Guy Jouas, our sound engineer, to tape as many of these sounds as possible and also to try to establish the relationship between a particular sound and the behavior of the animal making the sound. During the afternoon, he recorded six reels of elephant seal noises. There are a great variety of such sounds: snores, gurglings, barks like cannon shots, some like the firing of an automatic rifle, and, of course, the sounds of battle.

"The males," Guy explained to us, "place their trunks into their mouths to create a kind of resonance chamber. Their sounds are not really cries. They are rhythmic noises that remind me of the sounds of tom-toms.

"I have no idea why an animal will make a particular sound at any given moment. I have the impression that they are a means of asserting authority, a sort of proclamation which the male issues to his harem. Even the sounds made by the males in battle have the same curious, rhythmic tom-tom effect. And the challenge itself is not a continuous, harsh sound. It is deep, and rather sharp, and has a somewhat faster rhythm than the other sounds.

"I should add that the males are hardly ever silent. If the male in one group of animals makes a sound, those in the neighboring groups feel obliged to answer.

"There is a very noticeable difference between the noise made by an elephant calmly guarding his harem and that which he makes preparatory to a battle. The latter instance, I believe, is the only occasion on which the elephant seal shouts. It rarely does so during the battle itself, and never afterward whether he has won or lost the encounter.

"If a male stays a hundred yards or more from another male, there is no trouble. But if one comes out of the water near another male guarding his harem, there will probably be a battle.

"During the encounter itself, one hears the sound of the antagonists' bodies striking against each other. Although the wounds that they inflict do not seem very serious, there is always much blood.

"It is likely that in some cases the male elephant seal is merely trying to express himself, to affirm his authority and power. At least, that is my impression.

"I've listened to, and recorded, all the sounds that these animals make, but I have been unable to discover any indication of a language analogous, say, to that of the humpbacked whale."

Guy Jouas is a convinced champion of fem lib, and he noted that, at least among the animals, the females generally exhibit more sensitivity than the males. In this instance, he was unable to record any of the females' sounds, for it appears that certain female elephant seals are perhaps mute. They do not seem to take any interest in the battles of the males; or, in any case, they do not encourage the males by showing any interest.

The young animals, Guy reported, are very noisy. "Some of them scream in pain because they have been jostled or crushed. Others cry because they are hungry and their mothers have abandoned them. Their cries are quite loud, but they seem to have no effect. Their mothers do not answer."

Following Guy's report, I wished to try an experiment. I asked Eugène Lagorio and Canoë to walk along the beach, playing Guy's tapes of the elephant seal's challenge sounds. They waited until a male had come fairly close to a second male, then they turned on the tape. The two males, both of them obviously surprised, raised their heads and issued their challenges. When it seemed that the males had calmed down somewhat, Lagorio played the tape again. Soon, the two males were locked in combat.

I could not help being reminded of how equally easy it is to move human beings to violence, when, by means of well-orchestrated propaganda, hatred is created and sustained.

We have undertaken a whole series of observations with the elephant seals. We began by taking the measurements of animals of different ages. The elephants more or less gracefully allow us to do as we wish. Philippe is in

A female elephant seal has developed a crush on Serge Foulon

Left: As violent as their parents may be, young elephant seals have moments of tenderness

charge of this operation.

It requires patience and, above all, agility, to measure an animal weighing two or three tons. An elephant seal may attain a length of almost twenty feet. Its forward flippers are capable of crushing a man. The most difficult part, therefore, is measuring the trunk. It was not until the twentieth century that we knew the purpose of this appendage. It was once believed that the trunk was used as a means of underwater breathing, or that the elephant seal used it to pick up its food. The sailors we spoke to were convinced that the males used it to lure females to their island. The experts now agree, however, that the trunk's only function is to serve as a resonance chamber when an elephant seal issues a challenge.

Baby elephant seals are between three and four feet long and approximately thirty-six inches around their middle. Their undeveloped bodies are extremely supple. Their forward flippers are shaped like human hands and are about the same size as those of Philippe. As among all web-footed mammals, the phalanx is long but not disproportionately so. Much of the length of the paws is taken up by the long, stiff, cartilaginous points in which all of the fingers end. These points, which are quite visible, are not claws.

Beneath them, there are very short nails. The webbing joins the fingers and toes but does not go beyond the last phalanx.

I had intended to run an electrocardiogram of a large male; but several attempts all ended in pandemonium, with all the electric wires pulled out of the machine and the good doctor lying on the rocks.

The large male elephants are less indolent than we had first thought. In fact, they appear somewhat nervous. Though usually apathetic, these great hulks of flesh and fat are easily moved to anger. When one goes near them on the beach, it seems that nothing can disturb them, so accustomed have they become to our presence. But, suddenly, a male will rise and charge. They may move slowly and clumsily when they are making their way to and from the water; but when they attack they are quite fast despite their weight, and anyone in their path must beat a hasty retreat.

The way in which these animals move is reminiscent of land worms. Their bodies undulate, curve, and seem to push themselves forward, caterpillar-style. The elephant's oily skin wrinkles in successive waves. (This skin is not smooth and silken like that of dolphins, but rough and covered with hair.) They do not drag themselves on their forward legs but rather move the rear part of their bodies to the front. Then they arch their backs and push their heads and shoulders forward by bracing themselves on their rears.

A Celebration

Calypso was unable to remain at Guadalupe much longer, since we were scheduled to follow the migration of the gray whales along the Pacific coast. We therefore planned to leave a team to continue our observations of the elephant seals and, if at all possible, to film a mating and the birth of a calf.

As pressed as we were for time, I could not bring myself to leave our shipmates on this desert island at that particular moment. It was December 31, New Year's Eve. Everyone returned to the ship for the night, and we spent a jolly evening. Morgan, our chef, outdid himself; and we sang all the songs which have become traditional aboard *Calypso*. The singing and shouting were carried to the beach by the wind, and the elephant seals, kept awake by our racket, answered by roaring into the night.

The following morning, January 1, we made our preparations for departure. The team assigned to remain on the island consisted of Sumian, Jean-Clair Riant, and Yves Omer, who spent the first part of the morning loading supplies into a zodiac. These supplies included an impressive number of cases of canned goods. Morgan, apparently, had stripped our pantry for the benefit of the men we were leaving behind. He also confided his most infallible recipes to them — which is the ultimate accolade bestowed by Morgan on his special friends. There were also cans of film, cameras, binoculars, diving suits, scuba gear, and assorted other items to make life, if not comfortable, then at least bearable and productive on the black rock called Guadalupe.

A Social Upheaval

The team stationed on Guadalupe was able to confirm what I had sensed regarding the social life of the elephant seals. Their excessive overpopulation had indeed subjected them to abnormal living conditions and resulted in overaggressiveness. (There was, in other words, an obvious parallel to what is happening in our own cities, for the same reasons.) In Argentina, a few weeks later, we saw a large concentration of elephant seals on the Valdés peninsula. The peninsula is quite large, and the animals were much less congested than those at Guadalupe. Their territories were therefore sufficiently far from one another for the harem society to exist and for the encounters between males to retain their purpose, which is to defend their domains and their females. (However, the elephant seals we saw in Argentina were not of the same species as those on Guadalupe.)

On Guadalupe, on the other hand, the situation is critical. Not only does each male have to defend his territory against his immediate neighbors but also against males, both young and old, who frequently emerge from the water to invade his territory. The purpose of the latter is sexual. They want to couple with the females of the harem, who are fertile only for several weeks of the year. These marauding males are outcasts, rejected by society. They live on the fringes of the social structure and are always in search of a female and of a fight.

"You can see the young males trailing after the females," Yves Omer observed. "You can see the lust in their eyes. Sometimes it happens that the male will find a young female in the water and couple with her. Then they both return to the beach as though nothing had happened."

The battles waged between these outcast males and the protector of a harem may be distinguished from those fought between two equals in the hierarchy over their respective claims to be master of the beach. In the latter

Following page: A leisurely sunbath on the beach

case, the adversaries are sometimes a good distance apart, sleeping peacefully. They are usually of about the same size. Then, suddenly, one of them
rises and issues a challenge. The other animal answers. This exchange takes
place very quickly. Gradually, the antagonists move toward one another,
both of them stopping occasionally to lie down but roaring continually until
they meet in combat. Then, they hurl themselves against one another, chest to
chest, where their skin is much thicker then elsewhere on their bodies. Their
formidable teeth attempt to reach one another's trunks, and they protect
themselves against such assaults by pushing outward with their chests. Their
canine teeth are sufficiently long to cause serious damage, for they do not
really bite so much as use their teeth as sharp objects with which to stab one
another. (The only time they actually bite seems to be when one succeeds in
sinking his teeth into the other's rump.) The trunks of some elephant seals we
have seen have been cut to ribbons.

The battle almost always progresses from the beach to the water, There,
in the breakers, under the indifferent eyes of the females, the encounter becomes more furious, and the wounds inflicted are more serious. The thick skin
which serves to protect the animals' chests on land, provides only a minimum
of protection in the sea; though, because of the breakers, less blood is visible.

Very often, the battle comes to a halt as suddenly as it began. The vanquished elephant seal does not fight until exhaustion. Instead, he acknowledges defeat, and the victor spares him. Moreover, these animals are too
massive to be able to sustain more than fifteen minutes of combat. When it is
over, both animals return to lie on the beach, as though nothing had happened to disturb the routine of the morning. It almost always happens that
mating occurs immediately after such an encounter; as though, among elephant seals, it is natural for violence to end in love.

When the colony was less populous, a victorious male could expect to
reign in peace over his harem for the rest of the mating season. Now, however, he is subject to continuous challenges from other males, and it sometimes happens that a male who wins one battle will lose the next one.

The Love Life of the Elephant Seals

The male elephant seal is almost twice the size of the female. This difference, however, does not necessarily intimidate the females. They seem to
take a mischievous delight in running away from the males.

As one can imagine, the beach is a study in pandemonium when the
mating season begins among these animals. The laws of the harem no longer

obtain, and there is neither freedom of choice nor fidelity in the sexual relations of elephant seals. We have seen some females receive several different males on the same day. And the males, whether they have won or lost in personal combat, take any female indicated by chance.

So far as the male is concerned, the situation is not as idyllic as it may sound because the females are less eager than he for an undertaking which is far from easy for them. The male must therefore attempt to couple with several females in succession before he meets with success. Yet, he manifests neither impatience nor anger. Unruffled, he attempts to dominate his partner who, for her part, gives no sign of sharing his excitement and remains singularly unmoved by his attentions. The younger females seem inclined to submit, but the older ones sometimes rebuff the males.

The sex organ of the male is the size of a wine bottle in circumference, and about the length of a man's arm. It contains a penis bone.

We have often observed that when a male emerged from the water to approach a female, he seemed to be motivated by a sudden and strong impulse. He begins by placing his flipper on the female's neck, then leans on her with all his weight and tries to couple with her. It is a surprisingly tender scene, given the size of the animals involved.

"One morning," Yves Omer reports, "we saw young elephant seals couple together in the open water, in the shallows. It was a rather touching spectacle. The male had one flipper on the shoulder of the female, while, with the other, he was leading her and moving in time to her own movements. I don't think that anyone else has ever seen a moment of such tenderness in the sea. Nor had anyone suspected that elephant seals eventually would couple in the sea. Yet, we filmed such a scene."

Although the sexual urge seems to come suddenly upon males, its satisfaction is delayed for social reasons. The old masters of the harems defend their females jealously, and the younger males can hope only for occasional contacts.

Maternity

The female elephant seal is not an altogether ideal mother, but she does more or less meet her responsibilities — although she does not seem always able to distinguish her own offspring from other calves. She is very casual about nursing. Usually, she will allow her young to feed immediately after birth, but subsequent nursing sessions take place irregularly. Maternal love seems to be a major drive among elephant seals only in the few days follow-

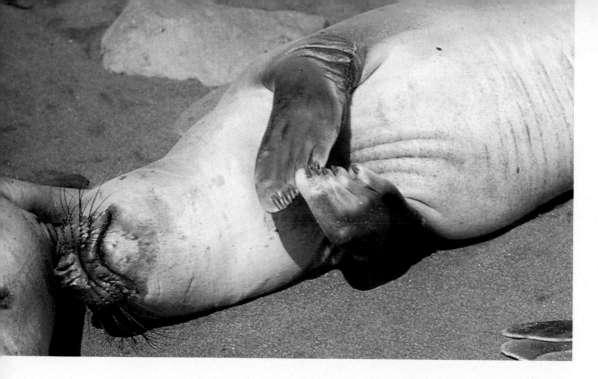

ing birth. Yet, there are exceptions to this rule. One mother attacked Philippe and Maurice when they attempted to take the measurements of her offspring.

The period of gestation, during which the female is mostly in the open sea, lasts for 350 days. When a calf is born, it is barely able to see and moves about only with difficulty among the fighting, mating adults. None of the adults seem to notice them, and a third of the young die during their first year of life.

Baby elephants drink about two quarts of their mothers' milk a day. The milk is particularly rich in fat, which allows the young to survive until they are strong enough, and skilled enough, to find their own food in the sea.

It is quite possible that the general indifference of the mother to her offspring is a consequence of overpopulation. Elephant seal mothers who bear their young far from the tumult, which obtains at the center of the colony, seem very inclined to protect their offspring.

By the time that *Calypso* left Guadalupe, the females had already begun to bear their young, and masses of placenta were visible on the beach. The mothers did not eat it, and sometimes the young elephant seal trailed it behind him until it was pounced upon and carried off by sea gulls.

As has already been mentioned, whenever a female goes into labor, she is immediately surrounded by the other females of the group. For this reason, our team was never able to film an elephant seal giving birth. It is also likely that the females usually bear their young during the night. We know for certain, however, that birth occurs on land rather than in the sea. A female bears only one calf at a time. At birth, the calf weighs thirty to forty pounds and measures about thirty inches in length. Like baby dolphins, young elephant

The gentleness and trust of young elephant seals is evident in their appearance

seals come into the world not head first, but tail first.

The calves are almost helpless, and absolutely charming. They are black, with a rather pointed head and maroon eyes. When they scratch, or make faces, they are quite engaging.

As they grow, they play at the edge of the waves, following the movement of the tides and trying their strength in the pools on the beach. They belong to a species which, some twenty million years ago, abandoned the

land for the sea. Therefore, they are not born swimmers but must learn to maneuver in the water. They teach themselves to do so, although sometimes the mother elephant seal will remain nearby during her offspring's first ventures into the water. It happens not infrequently that calves are carried out by the waves and drown. We have seen many of their bodies in the water along the shore.

Philippe and Canoë were able to save one drowning calf. The animal was still quite young, but it already weighed about fifty pounds. After pulling it out of the water, they examined the animal but could find no evidence of a wound of any kind.

The immediate problem was to locate the calf's mother among the thousands of females napping on the beach. Philippe decided to turn the calf loose and follow to see where it would go. It wandered from female to female, looking for one who would feed it. When females have milk, they will nurse any calf, but they must first feel the need to rid themselves of the milk. Otherwise, they remain deaf to the most heart-rending cries of a hungry baby.

Finally, the animal found a female willing to feed him, and when they left him, he was sucking away happily.

Baby elephant seals are weaned at the age of two months. They must then hunt for food in the sea, where, if they survive, they will spend three-quarters of their twenty years of life.

Wine for Lobsters

The stay of our three men on Guadalupe passed without incident. They occupied themselves with the elephant seal, dived, and explored the island. They were particularly struck by the contrast between the desolate island and the extraordinary wealth of vegetation in the water. A great mantle of algae covered all the submerged rocks, and the bottom to a depth of sixty feet.

It was not a simple undertaking to take a walking tour of Guadalupe. Two days were required for the complete trip. The men discovered a colony of seals living on the north side of the island, but they did not disturb the animals, since the film on which they were working was concerned only with elephant seals.

Life on the island was enhanced by a group of Mexican fishermen who pitched camp not far from our team's beach. The two parties were soon on excellent terms. The Mexicans fished for lobsters and exchanged them for some of the wine which Morgan had contributed to the team's store of supplies.

A New Team

When *Calypso* returned to Guadalupe after a week, our men were quite prepared to give up the noise, and especially the smell, of their elephant seals. It was now the turn of Philippe and Michel Deloire to try their hand at filming on shore.

Almost immediately, they found a wounded baby elephant and brought it back to *Calypso* to care for it. It was about six feet long and proportionately heavy, and it struggled constantly and attempted to bite. It was necessary to tie it down in order to bandage an ugly wound on its forehead. Then, we returned it to the island.

We now have almost all the material we need for the film. We have only to shoot some continuity footage, and to observe the elephant seals in the water, from our diving saucer.

Six

The Elephant Seals

Calypso returned to Guadalupe on January 31, and remained until February 6, 1969. We had only a week — hardly enough time to solve the mysteries presented by elephant seals; but it was the mating season, and a week was enough to afford us a peek into their lives at a critical moment.

The first group of elephant seals to arrive at Guadalupe were the great males, their coats grayish, rough, and covered with the scars of their many love battles. They were in rut, and their wrinkled trunks were rosy in spots and swollen with blood.

The females, coming ashore in Guadalupe to bear their young, arrived later. As soon as the calves were born, the males attempted to acquire the females for their harems. At the time that the young are born, there are approximately the same number of males and females. It would therefore be possible for couples to pair off without the necessity for combat — if the large males were not polygamous. But they are, and they monopolize the females. There are some bull elephant seals whose harems number over a hundred

Left: This female is angry because she was taken by surprise

females. Thus, all the young males are forced to remain celibate, relatively speaking.

I was particularly interested in seeing if it were not possible to tame an elephant seal and even to put a harness on one, as we had done with Pepito and Christobald. The idea of taming an animal weighing two or three tons and of letting it become familiar with divers in the water seemed to warrant all the trouble that we were taking at Guadalupe.

On the first day of our stay, we sent out three teams. One was a camera team which went ashore. The second was an underwater camera team. And the third was a special team assigned to the task of harnessing a good-sized elephant seal.

The special team did not have an easy job of it. The male struggled until he was able to escape, then turned, shook himself, and charged the men, using his head as a club. But the team did not give up. Bernard Delemotte finally succeeded in straddling the animal and was ready to buckle the harness over its body when the elephant arched its back, reared, and unseated Bernard. Then it fled. Or rather, it tried to flee, but it had been exhausted by the struggle, and the men had no trouble catching up with it again.

At this point, I called a halt to the proceedings. The elephant was obviously at the end of its strength, and it seemed unnecessarily cruel to continue. Moreover, it was obvious that the men of the team were in danger of being bitten by those massive jaws, or crushed under that mountain of flesh. How strange that these giants, who differ so radically in size and temperament from our sea lions, should be so fragile that they move us to pity.

The Mystery of the Trunk

The chief characteristic of the elephant seal, that which makes it a truly extraordinary animal, is its trunk. This organ is very reminiscent of that of the tapir and the elephant; and it gives the elephant seal the same air of secret embarrassment that I have noted in tapirs, as though in both cases the animal is conscious of carrying about a clumsy and somewhat useless accessory. And, in both cases, the trunk seems non-utilitarian, for it is never used for grasping objects. The elephants of Africa and India, on the other hand, have turned their trunks into instruments of marvelous dexterity, which enable them to perform the most delicate as well as the most violent tasks. They can grasp a coin as easily as they can demolish a tree.

What is the use of the elephant seal's trunk? The fact that it exists does not necessarily mean that it has a use. Many animals have organs that serve no purpose at all but are vestiges inherited from remote ancestors. Such organs exist only as evidence of an animal's past. And, in the past, there were many animals with trunks (or proboscidians, as they are known). In Africa, they go back some 50 million years.

The observation of elephant seals reveals that the trunk is found only among males and that it grows as the male ages. It is not merely a vestigial appendage. We have seen elephant seals place their trunks into their mouths, as I have already mentioned, in order to amplify their sounds. Unlike the land elephant, however, it cannot extend its trunk before it, or raise it above its head. Yet, like the trunk of its namesake on land, the trunk of the elephant seal is also a weapon.

In order to understand the use of the trunk, one must understand its shape. It is not a regular cylinder but flattens and tapers from its base on the elephant seal's forehead to its extremity. The extremity bears a vague resemblance to a paddle — or a club. And it is used as such. When a male encounters a rival, he rears up and brings his head down with tremendous force on his opponent, trying to stab the latter with his large canine teeth and, at the same time, to club him with the flat end of his trunk. The elephant seal's nostrils are located at the end of the trunk, but to the sides of it, and they are turned outward in such a way that they are not injured when the animal uses the trunk in this manner.

The elephant seal's trunk begins at the point where the snout of related animals, such as seals and sea lions, ends. Directly above the elephant seal's eyes, there is a round lump of flesh from which grow long whiskers. These whiskers reach a length of twenty inches, and they obviously play a tactile role, like the whiskers of seals or cats. They are the organs of mysterious senses which function on land as well as in the water, and they enable the elephant seal to perceive the presence of a living being — an enemy, or food — at a distance. The whiskers, therefore, are more than tactile organs. They play an important role in the animal's life and in its perception in all three dimensions.

The mouth is located under the trunk. It is soft and flaccid, and the lips are tender and sensitive.

A Leather Bag

We filmed and photographed the largest male specimens we were able to find so that we could study the more unusual aspects of the animal and so that we could familiarize ourselves with his gestures which, seen from close up, are quite surprising.

Philippe Cousteau engages in a somewhat violent dialogue with a large male

The grandfather elephant seal who was our subject seemed to be asleep on the beach, his eyes half-closed, his trunk hanging limp on the rocks. His forepaws, which seemed ridiculously small, were lying along his body, and his hind paws were stretched out behind. He looked like nothing more than a leather bag filled with jello — and not only filled but overflowing. The animal's soft body spread out, spilling onto the rocks around it, from its stomach.

This overflow results from the tegumentary texture of the elephant seal,

Life on Guadalupe allows much leisure to the female elephant seals

Bernard Delemotte pets a young female — and awakens the jealousy of the lord of the harem

which is similar to that of the walrus. Under a very thick corneous layer, there is a layer of fat which may reach a thickness of four inches. Between this layer and the animal's muscles are located the aponeuroses. It is not difficult to understand why the stomach of an animal wrapped in such an envelope of fat spreads out when it lies on the ground.

Our elephant seal's nostrils were raised slightly above the ground as we observed him, and from them issued a continuous litany of noises — snores, belches, and gargling sounds. Elephant seals have some very human habits. They are heavy snorers, and occasionally they sneeze. In fact, they seem per-

The two horizontal flippers of this young specimen are its hind limbs. The very short tail is visible between the two flippers

petually to have colds and runny noses.

In order to attract our elephant seal's attention, Bernard Delemotte gave him a hard but friendly whack on his hindquarters. Immediately, he reared up. It was an impressive sight. With only the forward third of his body in the air, his head was seven or eight feet above the ground. The neck and trunk were like a single, massive cone at the top of which an extraordinarily large mouth yawned — a mouth worthy of such an animal. A sound came, rhythmic, persistent, penetrating. It was a sound simultaneously of complaint, protest, and warning. I could not repress a feeling of pity in the presence of this giant who wanted nothing more than to be allowed to sleep in peace.

One of the most striking things about elephant seals is their method of locomotion. I have already described these animals as "crawling"; but they do not really crawl, in the sense that a caterpillar crawls — that is, by displacing the various segments of their bodies. Elephant seals are a single mass of flesh, a mass of muscle without an area against which to brace themselves. Their weight is such as to make it impossible for them even to pull themselves along on their forepaws. They are able to move only by rearing up, and then falling forward and, finally, moving their hindquarters forward to catch up with the rest of their bodies. This movement is dependent upon a series of contractions of the animal's muscles, or rather, a succession of violent spasms which seem to require a great effort on the part of the animal. Even so, it usually moves at a slower pace than that of a man walking at normal speed. But, if it is frightened, it is able to move more rapidly.

Elephant seals have been called the ugliest of the marine mammals. That is so only among those who have never had occasion to observe the grace and beauty of these animals in the water. Ugliness, like beauty, is in the eye of the beholder. So far as I am concerned, elephant seals are pathetic rather than ugly. There are even some aspects of their physiognomy that I find not unattractive. Their globular, sunken eyes, for example, often have an unexpected look of intelligence — a look which is different in the water from what it is on land. The eyes, which are usually brown, also convey sadness, and even supplication, when an elephant seal is disturbed on the beach and forced to fight, or to flee despite its crushing weight. In the sea, the animal's look is more alert than on land, and also more mischievous and more self-assured. It stares back at our divers without the slightest sign of fear or apprehension.

Following page: During the mating season, the elephant seals on Guadalupe do not venture far from shore

Our underwater camera crew was able to get some wonderful footage, thanks to the elephant seals' skill as divers and swimmers. They more than compensated for their awkwardness on land by their grace in the water.

The conduct of these animals in the sea is fascinating. They seem thoroughly at home, lying on their backs on the algae at the bottom in thirty or forty feet of water. They seem to have all the time in the world, or rather, all the air that they could possibly need. Lying on their backs seems to be their favorite position.

Our divers have carefully observed and filmed the swimming technique of the elephant seals. The two vertical flippers located toward the rear of their bodies move together in the same direction. In order to slow their speed, the animals spread these flippers, which function like the flaps of an aircraft.

Even *Calypso*'s divers are no match for these champion swimmers. When the elephants caught sight of our men approaching — their sight is excellent, and they have a broad field of vision in the water — they moved away, undulating slowly. It required only three swishes of their flippers for them to disappear completely in the distance. They are astonishingly supple. They turn back on themselves, circle, and perform any number of maneuvers. Then, when they rest on the rocks at the bottom, their bodies conform exactly to the shape of the rocks.

If one pities the elephant seals on land, as I do, then one must also envy them in the water. Their tremendous weight is neutralized then, and their bodies are no longer a curse. In the sea, they are in their true element.

To tell the truth, we have never met animals who have made the transition from land to water (sea lions, sperm whales, dolphins, etc.) without feeling a touch of envy. With all of our training and all of our technological resources, we cannot even come close to their performance in the sea. This is one of the reasons why it is our ambition to make these marine mammals our diving companions. They are experts.

We had two mishaps in pursuit of that ambition. Yves Omer was studying and filming a male in the water, in a large crevice in the rocks. He was getting some excellent close-ups against a background of algae moving gently in the swell, when an unusually strong wave pushed him toward the animal. The star of Yves' footage was startled and, his jaws yawning, charged the equally startled cameraman. Fortunately, no damage was done to either party. On the same day, however, a similar encounter had a somewhat less happy consequence: one of our cameras was crushed.

On another occasion, Sumian encountered an animal sleeping at the surface of the water. Being very careful not to awaken the animal, he was able to get close enough to it to tweak its whiskers — whereupon the outraged

Even in the water, elephant seals are irascible creatures

elephant gave a bound and disappeared. This is Sumian's favorite game. He has been bitten once, lightly, but he explains that, in that instance, it was because he had grabbed, not the whiskers, but the hind paws of a sleeping animal.

Pink Elephants

Shortly after the birth of their young, elephant seals molt. It is not a pretty sight, for the animals then become truly ugly and look as though they had some loathsome disease. Their coats fall off in sections, beginning with the head and ending at the tail. They grow out again, but the hairs are very short. They change not only their coats, but their skin as well, and no elephant seal leaves Guadalupe until its molt is complete. The beaches, therefore, are a pitiful spectacle. The animals, with their skin hanging in tatters, look like beggars in rags; moreover, they themselves seem to be embarrassed by their transformation into pink, flabby monsters, and they whine and groan continually. The smaller animals accelerate the molting process by rolling and rubbing against the rocks.

For most animals, molting is simply an unpleasant experience of brief duration. Among elephant seals, however, it is a veritable affliction which lasts for several weeks, and which causes the animals to suffer considerably.

Following page: Compared to one of these formidable animals, a diver seems small and vulnerable

Zoologists have noted that, during the molting, marine mammals run high fevers.

The Mystery of Food

Since we had been unable to harness one of the elephant seals, it occurred to me that we might at least be able to attach a buoy to a specimen, as we have done with whales. The buoy has the effect of slowing down the animal and makes it easier for us to follow it and film it in the water.

I was also interested in finding out what the elephant seals eat, and the buoy might make this possible. The Mexican fishermen believed that they fed on algae, and the sea around Guadalupe does, in fact, contain an abundance of vegetation. But we had never seen an elephant seal eat this vegetation, nor had we ever seen one of them eat a fish.

The teeth of elephant seals are sharp and widely spaced, which makes it possible for them to lacerate their food but not to chew it. It therefore appeared likely that they were obliged to swallow their food whole.

The bottom was also rich in abalones, but we had no reason to believe that the animals regarded these as edible. Most specialists, for that matter, are of the opinion that elephant seals abstain from food during the mating season.*

The first problem in attaching a buoy to an elephant seal is, obviously, to attach the buoy. It did not seem possible to use the same method that we had in marking whales, that is, to attach the buoy by means of a light harpoon which penetrates only the whale's layer of fat. I was afraid that this procedure, harmless as it is to whales, might cause serious injury to an elephant seal, which is somewhat less sturdy than a whale.

Philippe was able to come up with another method. He simply tied one end of a nylon line to the hind leg of a handsome male elephant and attached a red buoy to the other end. The animal, thrown into a panic by the line trailing behind him, rushed into the sea where our divers were waiting in a zodiac. A wild chase ensued. Rather than head for the open water, as we had expected, the elephant seal remained stubbornly among the rocks which lined the shore, dragging behind him the buoy which was bounding from rock to rock. It was only with great difficulty that the zodiac was able to follow the animal in its mad flight through this obstacle course, and then it did so only

---

*In the Kerguelen Islands, where elephant seals abound, they feed on squids, as evidenced by the beaks of the latter which have been found in the elephant seals' stomachs.

by ignoring the danger of hitting a submerged rock. Finally, the line broke, and the red buoy was thrown into the air and bounced up onto the beach. Naturally, that was the last we saw of our elephant.

This was going to be more difficult than it had seemed.

Next, we tried using one of our diving saucers to follow an elephant seal in the water, since we had noticed that they often dived in deep water and to depths where it was not possible for a human diver to follow. At such depths, an elephant seal is able to remain in apnoea for at least fifteen minutes. And, since it had occurred to us that elephant seals might feed only at night — which would account for the fact that we had been unable to observe them eating — we decided to make our trial run after dark.

The diving saucer — aboard *Calypso,* we call it the "sea flea" — was put into the water one night around midnight, with André Laban as its pilot. An hour later, it was hoisted back on board. André had discovered a leak, and his mission had to be aborted.

The next night, at 9 P.M., André tried again. First, he cruised over the fields of algae, where he observed several elephant seals — not eating, but sleeping. He then descended to a depth of between 250 and 300 feet, where the saucer's headlights picked up nothing more than a disordered mass of rocks and pebbles, strewn with empty abalone shells. These may have been the remains of an elephant seal's meal.

At that moment, the saucer's lights went out, and its engines came to a stop. André was in total darkness at 300 feet. However, his telephone was working, and he was able to contact us: "I am coming up. I have no more juice."

We immediately sent out a launch to pick up André and the saucer on the surface, but it was a dark night, and since the saucer had no lights, it was a long while before we were able to find him. (Since that time, our diving saucers have been equipped with electromagnetic signal devices.) Finally, André heard the launch's outboard motor and was able to guide us to his location.

The Elephant's Graveyard

Philippe, in one of his dives, had found a plateau of rock in deep water. On this plateau, there were a large number of elephant seal cadavers. It was an elephant's graveyard, of sorts, though not the one of which everyone speaks and which no one has ever seen. There were white skeletons over the whole stretch of it. It was a dramatic and striking sight in the dark depths of the sea, and we decided to record it on film.

Philippe took down a team of divers for that purpose. They first encoun-

Elephant seals, like humans, show their age. As they grow older, the flesh on their necks becomes more and more wrinkled

tered a number of bodies of elephant seal calves, floating at the surface or just below the surface. Then, the slow descent toward the elephants' grave-yard continued in silence and in growing darkness. A solitary shark, rising from the depths, passed the divers in sovereign indifference. From the socles

Below left: Sometimes, their noses run as though they had a bad cold

Below right: Elephant seals sometimes emit a deafening cry without apparent reason

A diver, accompanied by a minisub, tries to find out whether elephant seals feed on mollusks

of the volcanic isle, underwater terraces projected like balconies. The divers all experienced the same sensation: one of vague and increasing strangeness. In the darkness of the deep water, where the light of the sun was hardly visible, the surface seemed very distant. Life here was different, more oppressive, closer to death.

There was a final terrace. Then one of the divers switched on his light. All around the rocks, in nightmarish profusion, were the skeletons of the elephant seals, glimmering softly as the other divers switched on their own lights.

Meanwhile, near the surface, Louis Prezelin lighted an underwater torch and began his descent. The torch, spitting flames and smoke and leaving behind it an unearthly wake, was like a volcano erupting in the sea. In its ghastly light, the skeletons seemed to shiver and stir.

There is another mystery which one should perhaps elucidate. Since man has become aware of the existence of elephant seals, he has always been puzzled when he sees them on the beach, throwing sand, or algae, or even pebbles, with their flippers. There have been many explanations offered for this phenomenon: the animals are fanning themselves, or they are trying to rid themselves of parasites, or they are digging nests for themselves. None of these solutions is entirely satisfactory, and the mystery remains. It is aggravated by the fact that newborn elephant seals perform this mysterious scratching instinctively. It is not impossible that it represents the survival of a practice inherited from remote ancestors.

This scratching process is carried out with the animal's anterior flippers, which end in long, cartilaginous points. The points are used with surprising agility, and even elegance, when the elephant seal scratches. We had ample opportunity to observe this phenomenon, for the animals no sooner return to the beach from the sea than they seem overcome with an intolerable itch. Then, with their forepaws, they scratch their snouts, their necks, and, finally, any other part of their bodies. This scratching is made more mysterious by the fact that the elephant seal seems to have no parasites on its thick hide.

Quite literally, they scratch from birth to death. We have seen very small calves, lying next to their mothers, nursing, crying, and spending the rest of their time performing acrobatic feats in an attempt to scratch their heads and their backs.

April 4. The mating season has ended, and the elephant seals are already beginning to leave. At one end of the beach, the calves of ten or twelve weeks will live on their reserves of fat until they join the adults for the final departure *en masse.*

The calves are already quite large, for they grow fast. They also seem in good health. In order to be able to expend the energy necessary on this first sea voyage, a calf must have reached a weight of at least three hundred pounds, which means that it must have already consumed a ton and a half of milk in its short life.

The amount of milk which the females must supply is part and parcel of the mystery of feeding. If the females really do not eat, where do they get the calories necessary to produce so much milk? They do not seem even to lose weight during this ordeal of nursing. It is difficult to believe that the females take no nourishment in the five months that they spend on Guadalupe.

At Guadalupe, in any case, the abundance of yellowish excrement on the beach leads us to believe that, somehow, somewhere, the elephant seals must eat. On the other hand, there remains the fact that scientists who have dissected these animals have found their stomachs to be empty.

All we know from our own experience is that we have never seen an elephant seal taking food in any form.

April 10. Most of the animals of the colony have now returned to the sea. They remain in the waters around Guadalupe for a short while, as though they are warming up for a long trek across vast distances. The beaches are almost deserted except for a few animals at the edge of the water.

When the tide is low, we can see a large number of cadavers in the water, all elephant seals drowned in the past few months, and all young specimens. They also die on the beach, of disease and hunger, or they are crushed by the adult males. The older animals do not seem to die on land. They go to meet death in the immensity of the sea.

April 20. Calypso's watch has spotted several males who returned to the surface to breathe. For the first time, we are seeing elephant seals beyond the breakers of Guadalupe. They are obviously about to begin their annual maritime adventure.

The older, experienced males are the first to strike out for the open sea. *Calypso*'s launches have tried to follow them, but these animals are very fast swimmers, and, if necessary, they dive in order to escape our boats. It is hard to believe that these powerful, alert animals are the same apathetic giants we saw so recently on the beaches of Guadalupe.

The advance guard of older males will no doubt be followed soon by the whole population of the island.

The common life which we have shared with elephant seals seems, in retrospect, a long and moving story consisting of several stages. At the beginning, the animal seemed unattractive, even repulsive. Its monstrous body inspired little sympathy.

Yet, we ended by experiencing a real sympathy for these giants who are the victims of their own size. We discovered their virtues, their courage and tenderness, and love of freedom. And we were moved by the necessary violence of their lives, by the difficulties of their mating.

Their faces, at first, seemed inexpressive and even stupid. Later, we learned to read the whole range of emotions reflected there: tenderness for the females, the sweet pleasure of lying in the sun, rage in combat, hatred and defiance of one's rivals.

Somewhere in the dim recesses of time, the ancestor of the elephant seal chose to live in the sea. We, as divers — latecomers, certainly — noted and developed an intense admiration for their skill in adapting to aquatic life.

The drama of the elephant seal's life is not over. The animals are now totally protected by the Mexican Government, and they are multiplying rapidly. The beaches of Guadalupe, long their mating refuge, are no longer sufficient to contain them when, in the winter months, they return to land.

The elephant seals are therefore founding new colonies on beaches once frequented by their ancestors. Some of them have ventured even to the shores of Alaska. But, everywhere, they are encountering human civilization. In the sea off the California coast, they have fallen victim to oil pollution in the water. And, above all, man himself is everywhere, with his clumsy curiosity and his inadvertent brutality. Almost everywhere, the elephant seal is becoming the victim of the tourists, the gawkers, and the hunters who have returned to disturb the precarious peace which is indispensable to the survival of a newly founded colony.

The coasts of Alaska: green cliffs and glaciers

Calypso in the Bering Sea. The sea and the sky seem to be made of the same pale gray substance

PART THREE
Walrus

The bears of Kodiak Island are the largest in the world. They feed on salmon caught in the island's lakes and rivers

Seven

Calypso in the Bering Sea

After calling at San Francisco and Seattle, *Calypso* sailed from the latter port, in very bad weather, on a course for Anchorage, Alaska. We were on the first leg of a new expedition toward the Arctic, its route laying through the Aleutians and the Bering Sea.

A large part of our team had left us for a period of rest after six months of diving and strenuous effort, and they had been replaced by Albert Falco, Raymond Coll, Jean-Jérôme Carcopino, and several others who arrived ready for work.

It was June 1969. Springtime in Alaska.

As usual, our schedule was crowded. I had decided to make several films in the area: one on the red salmon, another on sea otters, and, finally, one of walruses.

In spring, the North Pacific is strikingly beautiful. We saw great cliffs, streaked by glaciers, plunging down to the sea, and islands covered with lichen. The sky and the water seem made of the same pale gray substance, and the landscapes are characterized by loneliness and a stillness touched with melancholy. The water is icy.

An expedition to Alaska is the kind of enterprise which is arduous while

Yves Omer, Jacques-Yves Cousteau, Albert Falco and Bernard Delemotte watch a school of salmon swim upstream on Kodiak Island

it lasts but of which, in retrospect, one retains a loving memory tinged, perhaps, with sweet sadness.

The country presents particular problems for a filmmaker. For one thing, there is almost no night; and the practical effect is virtual exhaustion. One can work with the camera twenty-two hours per day. And one sometimes did so,

A female salmon and a male (the latter is distinguishable by his rostrum or "beak") swim with all their might to reach the lake where they were born

with the result that our routine was totally upset. At six o'clock in the evening, we were still shooting. At 11 P.M., we began thinking about the sunset that we would film at midnight. And at 3 A.M., we began thinking about the dawn which we would not have missed for the world.

Salmon, Bears, and Sea Otters

We called at the port of Kodiak, a town curiously marked by its Russian past. There are churches with bulbous, gilded towers — a very turn-of-the-century czarist style. We even met bearded Orthodox priests in the streets, in their long black robes. It is sometimes hard to think of Kodiak as an American city and, in fact, Alaska did not become an American possession until 1867. The price paid for it by the U.S. Government was approximately equal to Alaska's present revenue from the salmon industry. The acquisition, although it was the subject of much ridicule at the time, has turned out to be a bonanza. Along with the millions of acres of ice and polar bears, which many people felt were Alaska's only resources, the United States acquired vast deposits of gold and oil. All in all, it was one of the bargains of history.

Kodiak Island, where we stayed for several weeks and where I eventually stationed a team headed by our chief diver, Albert Falco, was in the midst of salmon country. These fish, during the mating season, return to the lakes where they were born, swimming up the rivers and streams and leaping the cascades and waterfalls in a breath-taking exhibition of derring-do. Not all of these exploits end happily for the salmon. Bernard Delemotte has stood under these freezing waterfalls to catch them as they fell back exhausted and only half-conscious, from their attempts to scale the cataract, and then placed them in the water beyond so that they might continue their journey.

We also saw bears, the largest in the world, along riverbeds which were almost dry. These animals, sometimes thirteen feet in length, were fishing for salmon, using their paws to scoop a fish from the trickle of water and then, with a stroke of their teeth, cutting it in two. After a catch, the bear family — father, mother, cub — trudged off into the fields of wild lupines, where we could just barely make out their brown backs.

Along the lakes and streams of Kodiak, the worst enemies of *Calypso*'s men were not the bears but the ubiquitous mosquitoes which, in aggressiveness, ferocity, and taste for blood, at least equaled any the divers had encountered before. On several occasions, clouds of these insects literally engulfed our men and settled on their skins like a layer of coarse dust. It is said that the Alaskan mosquito will travel thirty miles in order to feast on the blood of a camper.

Sea otters use their hands to break open and eat mussels

Left: Salmon make prodigious leaps in their attempts to scale this waterfall. Many of them smash themselves against the rocks

Two Alaskan furred seals

In any case, it was necessary to take extraordinary measures for our men to protect themselves from these pests. Our cameramen and divers were equipped with hats shrouded in mosquito netting which fell to their shoulders. They looked liked a convention of beekeepers. As one can imagine, these hats and veils were not the most convenient apparel when it came to crossing a waterfall, or even eating a meal.

Unhappiest of all was Bernard Delemotte, whose face and hands were one mass of bites. He had challenged sharks with impunity, ridden bareback on whales, tamed moray eels, only to be vanquished finally by the mosquito.

When not battling the insects, we were on the lookout for the American, or bald, eagle which is the symbol of the United States of America. Like the bear, the eagle is a lover of salmon and is occasionally sighted in this area.

Unfortunately, the bald eagle is becoming increasingly rare and is classified as an endangered species. We saw none of these great birds.

The tour of the Kodiak region was not a simple matter. The divers were obliged to move on foot up small rivers with strong currents, dragging their zodiac behind them. They were constantly drenched by the waterfalls, some of them over sixty feet high, formed by the runoff of the melting snow. The power of some of the waterfalls we encountered while filming salmon was surprising.

Giant Crabs

Another revelation in store for us on Kodiak Island was the king crab, a crustacean the diameter of which, with its legs extended, sometimes exceeds three feet. A thriving industry has grown up around this formidable creature. It is widely fished, and modern canneries have been built to take care of the fisherman's catch. All around the island there are enormous traps, and trawlers return to dock laden with a cargo of struggling king crabs, their legs waving and their claws poised threateningly. There is the din of armor clicking, and, here and there in the squirming mass of reddish bodies, one sees a round black eye. It is a scene out of a science-fiction novel, and one which conveys an idea of the wealth and variety of life in the sea.

The canneries are, if anything, even more fantastic than their product. They are entirely white, like hospitals, and equally antiseptic. The gigantic crabs are carried on a belt between a blade and a man wearing a lead apron. The man, in a single motion, which he repeats a hundred times an hour, thrusts the crab under the blade. The blade kills the animal, opens it, and separates the flesh from the carapace. It is the equivalent of the slaughterhouses of Chicago except that, on Kodiak, the labor force is half Eskimo and half Japanese.

By all accounts, the commercial exploitation of the king crab has not yet endangered the species. Moreover, the waters around Kodiak are unusually rich, and this industry makes it possible for the Eskimos in the area to raise their standard of living and to find employment as fishermen and also to become owners of trawlers. It is not rare today to see a smiling Mongoloid face behind the steering wheel of a luxury automobile: an Eskimo who has made his fortune from king crab.

Our medical officer, Dr. Millet, was particularly interested in the crabs, and it was his heartfelt desire to witness a mating. We did everything we could to accommodate him, diving constantly and observing the crabs on every occasion, but it was not possible to find a pair mating. The doctor, however, drawing on his knowledge of crustacean anatomy, provided us with a vivid description of what such a coupling would be like if we were fortunate enough to witness it, and he made it sound as though it would have been a choice spectacle.

Despite the carapaces of the crabs, mating presents no particular difficulty because of the highly developed organs of both the male and the female of the species. One of the ten appendages of the male is its sexual organ, in which there is an ejaculatory canal. The sperm passes through this canal. The organ, which is segmented and articulated, ends in a small swelling, and it slides under the shell of the female, to the rear, and reaches the oviduct which is surrounded by a ring of hair. The male's copulatory arm then literally sweeps the oviductal orifice and deposits its spermatozoids within. As Dr. Millet said, "It is a simple act of coupling and quite interesting to visualize."

Among the Islands

Calypso left Kodiak Island on July 4 and sailed along Simeonof and Cherni islands. Jean-Paul Bassaget, *Calypso*'s captain on this occasion, suggested that we drop anchor in a relatively shallow area — in about sixty-five feet of water — and begin diving. We accepted his suggestion on two counts: first, these areas are often the habitat of a particular kind of marine life and therefore are worth a visit; and, second, it is always a good idea to have a "shake-down dive" for a new team before formally embarking on a specific

Following page: A crowd of walruses sunning themselves on a Round Island beach

project. We therefore dropped anchor, and Michel Deloire (with his camera), Jean-Jérôme Carcopino, Louis Prezelin, Jacques Delcoutère, and Dr. Millet slipped into the choppy, somewhat cloudy water. A zodiac was launched, to stand by in case of need.

There were large clouds drifting across the horizon as we waited. After a quarter of an hour, one of the divers returned to *Calypso* carrying a gigantic red starfish with blue arms, weighing perhaps twenty-five pounds.

The divers then appeared on the surface, one after another, each one carrying a similar trophy. We placed them all in vats, and Michel Deloire filmed close-ups of their wriggling arms covered with erect suction cups and tube feet.

In the wardroom, everyone was enthusiastic about what they had seen: a bottom pullulating with starfish — hundreds, perhaps thousands of the animals piled up, all of them enormous. "When they move," Michel Deloire reported, "they're like some incredible lawn mower. Everything in their path is devoured." But Michel had been disappointed in his plan to film the starfishes. There was a rather strong current, and the cloudiness of the water made it impossible for him to use his camera. We therefore decided to remain at anchor overnight and try a longer dive the next day.

As it happened, we remained where we were for the next thirty-six hours. During the night, a storm arose and we were tossed about quite badly. The anchor dragged, and *Calypso* began to drift in the wind. We had to start up our engines to regain our anchorage. By dawn the weather was still bad, and we abandoned our plans for another dive. The following day, although the water was still very rough, we sent a pair of divers down on a reconnaissance mission. They returned to report that there was not a single starfish to be seen on the bottom.

If there is a lesson in this entire episode, I suppose it is that, despite all our technological gadgetry, we are as much at the mercy of the elements when we are at sea as the most primitive tribesman in the Pacific. Eventually, one resigns oneself to Neptune's whims, but sometimes I cannot help wondering how many extraordinary films we have missed because of such bad luck. This was one such occasion. Starfishes are fascinating animals, and I have every hope someday of devoting a film to them.

A Garden of Life

We tend to think of the arctic region as devoid of life. We even speak of the arctic "waste." Actually, despite the harsh climate and the rigorous living conditions, there are a large number of life forms in the Arctic. In fact, it is in the cold northern waters that we find the largest concentrations of marine mammals.

Even more surprising is the presence of vast flocks of birds on the islands of the Bering Sea. There are literally millions of them, forming what may well be the largest concentration of birds in the world. Every rock of the Aleutians serves as a perch for them, in numbers that I have never seen equaled in any other part of the earth. Sometimes, a single species has colonized a rock and defends it against all other species. Sometimes, two species coexist peacefully on the same rock, with each species keeping to its own well-defined territory. Petrels and auks are there, living from the wealth of the sea. And there are gannets, or boobies; cormorants; gulls; terns; and puffins; all filling the air with their screeching. They are the undoubted lords of the islands, and most often they did not bother to flee even when we landed on the islands where they had their nests and raised their young.

Our mission at this time had nothing to do with birds, but no account of that mission would seem complete without at least a note of their existence. What was most striking was the incredible multitude of them, especially on the deserted islands we visited in our search for sea otters.

Sea Otters

The sea otter has been supplied by nature with a coat of surpassing beauty. This was a great misfortune for the animal, for its coat is counted among the luxury furs of the world of fashion, and, as a result, the sea otter is well on its way to extinction. The hunting of the sea otter is now prohibited, but poaching is widespread because, given the vast area involved, proper surveillance is extremely difficult.

That vastness, as detrimental as it may be to the sea otter in some respects, was a source of endless delight to us. There were animals without number along the entire Aleutian chain of islands. In the sea, there were kelps the stipes of which were as thick as a man's arm and 150 feet in length.

But it was not all delightful. The kelps were indeed something to be admired; but they also created problems for us, since they were constantly becoming entangled in our propellers, and our divers had to go down and clear them away.

These forests of kelp are the hiding place of the sea otter, that most graceful of animals. There have been times when we have had as many as twelve more or less tamed sea otters living aboard *Calypso* at one time. We

Calypso sends a team of divers ashore in a Zodiac

used to fill our small boats with water for them to use as pools on *Calypso*'s rear deck, and the divers fed them by diving for large, red-fleshed mussels. There is nothing more entertaining than watching a sea otter eat a mussel. It floats on its back and holds the mussel on its chest while trying to open it with its tiny hands. On their own, they find a stone on the bottom and use it to break open the shell. Aboard *Calypso,* we provided stones and were surprised at the dexterity of the sea otters in opening the shellfish. Then, as sea otters are very clean animals, they washed themselves as carefully and as continually as cats do.

Most of the walruses we saw on Round Island were males. Many of them had one tusk broken

A full-grown walrus is a somewhat shapeless animal by human standards. It has no neck, and its head sits squarely on the trunk of its body

They were a source of endless interest to us. As soon as a sea otter's head was above the water and its silver whiskers were standing, it placed its hands on its cheeks or on its head and began swimming around on the surface. Sea otters also have the habit of stroking their fur, which serves the purpose of introducing air into their coats. The air provides insulation against the cold. The body temperature of the sea otter must be maintained at no less than 100°F., for it is a mammal, a warm-blooded animal whose ancestors once lived on dry land — like the pinnipeds and the cetaceans.

Their habits are so engaging, and their curiosity so open, that we finished by concluding that the sea otters of Alaska were among the most endearing animals we had ever encountered. They use their hands to rub their eyes or their stomachs in a very human manner, while looking at you questioningly. When they are among the kelps, they push aside the algae with their hands, like old ladies behind lace curtains, to stare at divers. They cradle their young in their arms, and when they nurse their offspring their gestures and attitudes are undeniably feminine. So as not to be carried away by the current, they anchor themselves to the bottom by tying a piece of algae around their waists.

We had several surprises in our search for sea otters in the vicinity of the Aleutians. One morning a team went out in a zodiac to explore an inlet, and Dr. Millet noticed a black mass floating in the water. It was a young seal not more than six or seven months old, asleep at the surface. He petted it, very gently. The seal awoke, opened one eye and looked at him, then fled in terror.

Our admiration for the sea otters of Alaska encouraged us to make several dives into the marine jungle of kelp where they live. The development of these algae is extraordinary. Their thallus is supported by floats. The central stem, as big around as a large bamboo, descends vertically into the darkness to a depth which sometimes exceeds one hundred feet. We have tried following the stem and were unable to find the lower end of it. Kelp is surely the longest, if not the tallest, vegetable life form on earth.

In relatively shallow water, where we were able to locate the base of the plant, the algae was fixed to the bottom by means of a holdfast attached to a rock. It is a fairly precarious anchorage, for these holdfast are not comparable in size to the roots of large trees on land. After all, they are not buried in the earth, and they derive no nourishment from the ground.

This weaving, rubbery, deep-shadowed jungle of kelp is the favorite haunt of the sea otters. There they find a hiding place from their enemies, and especially from man. But they also take shelter on land, on the banks of the islands, in order to find protection from the storms which sweep across the Bering Sea with winds of over a hundred and twenty miles an hour.

We put ashore at one of these islands to remain for several days and found it inhabited by an abundance of seals and birds. Our mission, however, was to observe the sea otter, and, for that purpose, we stretched a large net over the entry of an inlet. Our plan was to capture one of the animals and use the enclosed inlet as a natural tank, where the sea otter could remain in semi-freedom and where we could study its habits.

Since sea otters are very timid creatures, we decided to try to capture one at night. A team remained on watch, in one of the tents, throughout the hours of darkness. At the slightest noise, they came running out with their large diving lights.

We did see one sea otter at that time. It presented itself, quite openly, in our camp and even entered the watch tent and allowed itself to be petted. We were astonished at its boldness — until we discovered the reason: it was sick and had come looking for help. Dr. Millet examined the animal and discovered that it had an internal abscess which, unfortunately, was inoperable. The sea otter died a week later, and an autopsy confirmed our medical officer's diagnosis.

In the Bering Sea

On July 22, we cruised northward and entered the Bering Sea, dropping anchor near a rocky peak rising from the sea. It was not very high, and we could see lava flows on its sides. Patches of low grass were scattered about. This was Round Island, in Bristol Bay.

Michel Deloire had reconnoitered Round Island by helicopter and reported that it housed a large colony of walruses. Michel had seen hundreds of them, scattered over two rocky beaches.

Late in August, *Calypso* anchored off Round Island and sent a party ashore. There were only a few dozen walruses left on the island. The others had all disappeared. I was very disappointed. After our film on sea otters, our schedule called for one on walruses. Michel Deloire swore a mighty oath that there had truly been hundreds of the animals on Round Island only a short time before. We sent our zodiacs and launches to explore the other islands in the area. There were no walruses there, either, nor any sign of them. We could not imagine what had happened to them, and we never did find out. However, the next morning, Michel's eyesight was vindicated. We looked toward Round Island, and the beaches were colored brown by the animals, who had now returned as mysteriously as they had disappeared earlier. As we watched, they grew in numbers, until there were at least a thousand of them. They remained there for the entire period of *Calypso*'s stay.

We went ashore every day, divided into teams and distributed among our zodiacs and launches. It was our intention to film the walruses both on the beach and in the water.

Round Island is not easy to approach because of the rocks and the breakers. The only place our boats could land was on the beaches, and our arrival always caused the walruses to flee into the water. They gave every sign of being thoroughly frightened of humans. Well they might. The walrus has been hunted mercilessly, and still is, for its tusks. Walrus ivory is greatly esteemed and brings a high price. As soon as we landed, we found the bodies of two decapitated walruses. They had been killed no more than a week earlier.

Whenever one of our boats landed on the beach, there were always two or three hundred walruses already in the water. They seemed much more timid than the elephant seals had been, even though they are almost as large as our friends on Guadalupe. They remained in the water, just off the beach, in groups, diving, returning to the surface — and watching us constantly.

The habits of the walrus are somewhat more attractive than those of the elephant seal. For one thing, there is not the terrible odor that we had had to endure at Guadalupe, nor was there excrement on the beach. And, other than the walruses killed by hunters, there were no cadavers. The beach, in fact, was quite clean. Nor was there the unceasing din, the roars and screams, which had always hovered over Guadalupe.

At that time, there was very little happening on Round Island. It was not the mating season, and there was no combat to speak of. Occasionally, the animals engaged in minor hostilities over a particular piece of rock in the

The white tusks of the walrus are in strong contrast to its rosy skin

sun — for they love to nap in the sun, like retired clerks on pensions — but these involved nothing more than some groans and pushes and a few swipes in the air with their tusks. These were not duels but postures of intimidation.

Apparently, walruses do not molt. Their skins were thick and rosy, and the whiteness of their tusks contrasted with the color of their bodies. Seen from a distance of fifty or sixty feet, they seemed to be lined up in ranks and in groups, with all of their tusks in parallel lines and of approximately the same length.

These two walruses have each lost one tusk

We eventually came to know the walruses better in the sea than on the beaches. Their faces are strange but not repulsive. Their small round eyes look at one from the sides of their heads, and their wrinkled chins rise at a slant between their tusks, resembling nothing so much as brushes covered with stiff bristles. The smooth, round head sits squarely on the body. And, where the two join, there are folds of skin. There is no neck.

Their eyesight is not very good, but their sense of smell is excellent. They are rather easy to approach, so long as one takes the direction of the wind into account. But they are much less tolerant of humans than the elephant seals were. It is impossible to touch them, let alone to tame them. They flee at the slightest provocation, their bodies undulating, and pull themselves along on their forward flippers.

In the sea, on the other hand, we were able to come quite close to them in the zodiac without being attacked. This was unexpected, for we know that, in the Far North, in the midst of the floes, they often attack the boats of the Eskimos.

We would have liked very much to get some footage of the walruses feeding on the bottom. There is still some debate on their method of feeding. Until recently, zoologists believed that they used their tusks to dig in the sand or the mud for mollusks, especially clams, which they then crushed between their powerful molars. But an American specialist in the mammals of the arctic and antarctic regions, Dr. Carlton Ray, believes otherwise. Dr. Ray has examined the contents of the stomachs of many walruses, and he has never found any trace of shells. He therefore believes that the walrus feeds on animals which are not as difficult to eat as mollusks — starfish, for example, and

Walruses seem to like to huddle together at the very edge of the water

ascidians. For these, it is not necessary for the walrus to dig with its tusks. The tusks, therefore, would be nothing more than accidents of nature, like the "horn" of the narwhal. (It would be difficult to argue that the tusks are intended to be used as weapons in the mating rivalries of the males, since the female walrus also has them.)

It is known, in any event, that walruses are in the habit of swallowing small pebbles. It may be that they do so to facilitate digestion, or it may be that the pebbles relieve their hunger during their migrations.

I had called Round Island a "haven for the aged," because, as we visited there, I noticed that its inhabitants were mostly older males who probably could not follow the rest of the colony in its traditional migration to the north. When we were there, there were no young animals, and no females, on the island.

However, Dr. Carlton Ray has visited Round Island during the winter, and he has seen both females and young walruses. We must therefore conclude that Round Island is not an old-folks' home for the entire year. It is a port of call for migrating walruses and the permanent residence of the old males. Walruses, unlike elephant seals, are not great swimmers. And, unlike the latter, they do not swim great distances. When they migrate, they allow themselves to be carried by the currents, or they hitch rides on passing slabs of ice.

The rosy color of the Round Island walrus contrasts strongly with the maroon of the walruses farther to the north. The pinkish color of the old males, however, is probably due not to age, but to their exposure to the sun, for they are true sun worshipers. It was summer, and we were to the south of the Bering Straits. We were not surprised to note that the walrus was subject to sunburn and sunstroke. They actually turned red.

In exploring Round Island, we found two dead walruses, both with pairs of very handsome tusks. They had been shot by hunters, but only wounded, and had sought shelter in the sea. Then, as in the case of all mammals, their bodies had washed up onto the beach.

"Using a very sharp knife," Dr. Millet relates, "I tried to remove the penis bone, but I was unable to cut through the skin. I therefore opened the stomach, through the sexual orifice. I found a very thick layer of fat, and, finally, a mucous tube within which was the bone.

"This bone ends in a cartilaginous zone held in place by a tripodal ligament attached to the hipbone. The muscle is four or five times the size of the human bicep. It pivots the bone on the ligaments, causing an erection, and the penis emerges from the mucous tube.

"The odor throughout the dissection was almost unbearable.

"It took three days for me to open the head with a handsaw. I opened the skull at the level of the forehead. The bones are so thick that there is very little place left for cervical matter."

The cranial development in the walrus is minimal, and its sensory equipment is mediocre. The sense of touch, however, is quite well developed, thanks to the animal's "whiskers," which are actually well-vascularized and nerved vibrissae and which probably make it possible for the walrus to find its food in the sea. Also, despite the small size of its brain, the walrus seems capable of greater discernment and sometimes of affection than the elephant seals which we have observed.

This first contact with walruses did not, I confess, greatly endear the animals to us. Their bloodshot eyes, their hostile and lugubrious appearance, heavy jaws and corpulence are not very engaging characteristics. We had to keep reminding ourselves that walruses are not made for the sun and for verdant lands like Round Island. It was our misfortune, perhaps, to encounter them for the first time in a habitat which was not completely suited to them. The walrus is, in fact, a polar animal, at home in very cold water and, above all, among the ice floes. In such conditions, they are able to dive to almost two hundred feet, and to remain for five to fifteen minutes without coming to the surface to breathe.

Their faces, characterized by a comical gravity, are decorated with whiskers. Their thick, supple lips make it possible for them to take hold, with surprising delicacy, of the flesh of the very different animals on which they feed. It is said that a walrus can even eat the flesh of a fish and leave the bones intact.

Their massive heads, in which Dr. Millet noted the thickness of the bones, may contain an undersized brain, but it also allows them to break through thick ice during the winter. And their most effective weapons are their tusks, which are practically unbreakable.

We decided to move farther northward, into the glacial regions, in order to film these animals in their own element, in the Arctic. At the same time, we would take advantage of the opportunity to visit the last men whose lives are bound up with those of the walruses.

The walrus's favorite means of transportation is to hitch a ride on a floating island of ice

The Eskimo village of Gambell on St. Lawrence Island

Eight

An Island of Ice

In order to film the walrus in its natural, arctic habitat, I sent a team northward, to the entry of the Bering Straits, on a reconnaissance mission.

This team, comprising Ron Church, Louis Prezelin, and François Dorado, left by air from Los Angeles on May 1, 1970, for Nome, Alaska. At Nome, they bought supplies and such equipment as they would need to protect themselves against the cold. They had left Los Angeles in sunshine and balmy weather. When they landed at Nome, it was snowing. The sea was still cluttered with blocks of ice.

From Nome, they continued on by air to Gambell, on St. Lawrence Island. It was still snowing, and the temperature hovered between 13°F. and 18°F. St. Lawrence is rather large, about fifty-five miles in length, and is situated two hundred miles from Nome, about midway between Alaska and Siberia. Every winter, starting in the middle of November, it disappears entirely under a mass of ice and snow. St. Lawrence is a special victim of the cold. In 1970, for instance, the winter lasted unusually long. The thaw had not yet set in by the beginning of May, whereas it generally begins sometime in April.

It is hostile terrain so far as human beings are concerned, but it is hospitable to the walrus, that amphibious, migratory, and giant seal who reigns as uncontested master in the polar solitude, filling the icy air with its lonely, somehow pathetic, cries. The walrus is no longer found anywhere other than in the Arctic Ocean, in the neighborhood of the Bering Straits, and to the north of Greenland.

Every year, during the month of May, a strong ocean current carries great blocks of ice northward, from the coasts of Siberia and from Bristol Bay. These icebergs pass St. Lawrence Island, cross the Bering Straits, and reach Point Barrow, which is the northernmost point of the ice's retreat during the summer.

Most of the animals who spend the winter on the ice floes and who live at Bristol Bay make use of these floating icebergs on their summer trek northward. And, in the fall, they also use them as floating flatcars, moving in a current which flows southward, to carry them to places where they may find food during the winter.

It is impossible to reach St. Lawrence by boat until July. It is difficult even by air because of the fog, the snow, and the strong, sometimes violent winds. Nonetheless, airplanes occasionally brave the elements to carry supplies to the Eskimos who live on St. Lawrence, and who are now much less isolated than they were formerly.

The largest settlement on the island is Gambell. It consists of one street, lined with about fifty houses. There is another settlement on St. Lawrence, where the Eskimos also live by hunting walruses.

Once on St. Lawrence, our team had difficulty getting started on their reconnaissance mission. Their Eskimo guide, who had been hired by mail, had apparently found a more lucrative employment, and by the time our men arrived he was no longer available. Fortunately, Ron Church and his friends were able to locate another Eskimo, Vernon Slwooko, who not only took his responsibilities very seriously but also turned out to be our most reliable adviser and a featured player in our film.

A Land of Wind and Snow

It was so cold at Gambell that, during the first few days, no work could be done. The wind was from the northwest and carried great gusts of snow. There were times when, because of these gusts, it was literally impossible to see more than a few feet before one's face. There was no sun, and when the sky was visible through the snow, it was laden with heavy gray clouds.

Vernon, our guide, was able to put our team up at his house for a moderate charge. This house consisted of a single large room on the ground floor, which served Vernon and his family — his wife, their two young boys, and an infant who had been adopted — as a combination living room, dining room, bedroom, and bathroom. (Vernon and his wife have other children, but these were at school on the mainland.) There was a guest room on the second floor, where Church, Prezelin, and Dorado slept, surrounded by piles of diving equipment, underwater cameras, diving suits, and so forth.

The meals prepared by Mrs. Slwooko were consistently good, given the limited variety of food available. I do not mean to infer that our men were kept on the diet traditionally attributed to Eskimos: filet of walrus or polar-bear cutlets. It was much more convenient for Vernon and his family to eat, and to serve their boarders, food that came by air from the continental United States, such as frozen meat and dried beans. There really was very little of the exotic about Mrs. Slwooko's cuisine.

Until May 10, the bad weather continued unabated. Snow, wind, and clouds were the order of the day, every day. In this part of the world, the weather is the major factor in human activities. The cold, the wind, the storms — these are things to which humans must submit humbly, since they are natural phenomena which ignore our very existence. There were days, therefore, on which our men were unable even to leave the house, let alone attempt to dive. Then, suddenly, the temperature began to rise. The sun broke through, and a fairy-tale landscape was revealed: snowy mountains appeared, and ice glistened in the unexpected light. The midnight sun shed its constant rays, pink and gold, on the immense white plain and on the blue sea noisily bordered in silver by great blocks of ice in constant collision against one another.

On May 11, the wind fell. The temperature rose to 26°F. At 5 A.M., Vernon awoke the divers and explained, in an English which was barely intelligible (when the Eskimo and the three divers attempted to communicate in English, the result was bare intelligibility), that everything was ready for an inaugural venture into the sea.

The three men rose hurriedly and gathered up their equipment, trying to omit nothing they might need in their confrontation with the waters of the Arctic. They were conscious that this would be their first experience with that world of ice so hostile, and sometimes so fatal, to man.

Carrying their cameras, lights, and tanks of compressed air, they hurried to the shore. The entire village, it seemed, had gathered on the beach to contemplate the ice which formed a wall around Gambell; a wall which, for all its precariousness, seemed unscalable as the waves that crashed against it.

To venture out on the water in such conditions seemed little short of collective suicide. Nonetheless, Ron, Louis, and François, following Vernon's example, took their places in the boat. The boat — an *oumiak,* as the Eskimos call it — was a simple wooden frame over which walrus skins had been stretched, not more than eighteen or twenty feet in length. On this occasion, it was loaded with the divers' equipment. Vernon was at the water's edge, in his oumiak, and, at his signal, the divers climbed into their places. Vernon's sole concession to civilization had been to replace the oumiak's sail with a small outboard motor. Thus equipped, the craft put-putted out into the waves and headed northward.

The Walruses

It had been comparatively easy to keep warm during the preparations on the beach. Now, however, on the water, in the dense fog and the wind, forced to remain motionless in their boats, the three divers were chilled to the bone. It did not make their plight more bearable when they observed that the water around them was filled with oumiaks, their Eskimo occupants excited, joyful, racing their small craft against one another, as though they were on a pleasure outing. Actually, despite their gaiety, the Eskimos were at work. The first walruses had been sighted in the sea, and the news had, as always, been the occasion for much rejoicing in the village.

The icebergs were frightening enough without the fog. They floated sixty or seventy-five feet above the surface, and sometimes the oumiak was almost on them before they were visible. Then, Vernon, totally unruffled and without slowing his motor, executed a few dexterous maneuvers and skirted around them. It seemed that, at any minute, the icebergs — already undermined by the thaw — would certainly come tumbling down and crush both the oumiak and its occupants. Ron Church clutched his camera tightly to his chest, and Prezelin and Dorado tried as best they could to protect their photographic equipment against such an eventuality.

Vernon Slwooko, unmindful of the condition of his clients, continued on, a vague smile on his face. Our men took some comfort in the thought that, after all, their guide seemed to know exactly where he was going in the midst of all these obstacles. They kept one eye on his wake, as it traced his route through a sea the color of lead. The other eye was turned toward the islands drifting past, in the hope of spotting a walrus.

Thirty miles from Gambell, a group of black spots appeared on the surface of the sea. Slwooko slowed and carefully approached one of the spots, which seemed strangely humped. It was a mother walrus, carrying her calf on her back. Around her, other walruses were swimming lazily.

The midnight sun over the Arctic

As Vernon watched, an undecipherable smile on his face, the divers hastily suited up and began sorting out their equipment. They glanced at the water and immediately understood Vernon's smile. The water was black and cloudy, the sky without light. It would be impossible to take any shots or to get any footage beneath the surface. Moreover, the mother walrus and her calf were already far off, and the accompanying herd was beginning to disperse. It would be very difficult to film them in the open water, and it was decided to try to surprise them as they slept on the ice.

A layer of gray-white fog, its underside black against the sea, was suddenly split by icebergs and moved toward the oumiak as the wind quickly increased in velocity. Now, Vernon, still imperturbable, made a half turn and began heading back toward Gambell. How he expected to find his way through the fog and rough sea, with icebergs rising like ghosts on every side, was beyond our team's comprehension. They could only hope.

The icy water, thrown by the wind, soaked through the divers' clothing, their gloves, and even their diving suits. It bit their faces and any other exposed flesh. As the men crouched down to protect themselves, Vernon remained upright facing them, his eyes squinting into the distance, his shirt open on his brown, muscular chest.

Four and a half hours later, Gambell was before them. The oumiak was dragged across the wall of ice, and the men hauled their equipment over the remaining blocks as they slipped and slid over the moving chunks of ice. They arrived at Vernon's house with hands and feet numb and muscles stiff.

Until May 16, foul weather hung over St. Lawrence like a curse. The men were blown by the wind, crushed by the blackness of the sky, paralyzed by the cold, imprisoned by the sea which beat relentlessly against the wall of ice. Then, on the seventeenth, the sun peeked out. The clouds parted, and blue sky appeared. Immediately, the divers decided to go into the water at the edge of the ice, merely "to see," as they put it.

The entire population of the village followed them to the beach, with amused curiosity and, it must be admitted, more than a trace of incredulity evident on their faces.

The dive was something of an ordeal. The temperature of the water was 28°F. Visibility was not more than two or three yards, and a thick fog, created by the thaw, hung over the water. Nonetheless, Prezelin filmed some close-ups of jellyfish in the water. Then, he went to the bottom, about sixty-five feet beneath the surface, where he shot a group of crabs. Naturally, there were no walruses. So near to Gambell, the men had not expected to find any. All in all, they concluded, it was a poor return for so uncomfortable a dive.

At that point, one of the men glanced upward and saw what appeared to be a thick black veil overhead, at about the level of the surface. Before them, the divers saw nothing but a greenish darkness. They regrouped and began the ascent to the surface. A thick, hard layer of ice spread above them like a pall. Without their being aware of it, a swift current had swept them underneath this opaque and impenetrable ceiling. By moving toward the light, they were able finally to reach the open water; and the chaos of ice surrounding Gambell, when it appeared, seemed strangely to represent home and safety to the men.

A Success

On May 19, the team attempted an outing with Vernon. The sea was more calm, even though the fog remained and made navigation hazardous. The Frenchmen and the Eskimo by now had succeeded in communicating more satisfactorily by using rudimentary English combined with sign language. Dorado asked Slwooko how he was able to navigate in such conditions. The Eskimo, laughing, pointed to his nose. The mysteries of "smellometer" navigation were obviously an open book to him.

Once more, after several hours, our men reached the tentative conclusion that they were wasting their time. It seemed doubtful that they would sight any walruses. And, even if they did, it was debatable whether their equipment would be able to function properly in the cold and the dim light. The fate of their mission, as well as their lives, was in the hands of their guide. For the first time, the men felt helpless in the sea and completely at the mercy of another man.

Suddenly, Slwooko increased his speed almost imperceptibly. He had seen something as yet invisible to his companions. Then, they saw it also: a white glare on the horizon which signaled the presence of a long layer of ice. As the oumiak moved closer, Vernon spoke, and his words were carried by the wind: they were very close to Soviet territory, probably less than ten miles from Siberia.

The men were now close enough to the island of ice for them to be able to see what they had been looking for. Each block in the long, broken bank was occupied by one or more walruses. They could see several mother walruses, half-rampant over their sleeping calves. Slowly, carefully, Slwooko took his oumiak past the animals and pointed out a peculiarity of one of the mother walruses. Her tusks were quite long and curved sharply inward, so that they crossed under her chin. This was obviously a dental anomaly. Ordinarily, the tusks of females curve gently inward toward one another. Only the tusks of the males are straight.

Left: Our Eskimo guide, Vernon Slwooko

Right above: The oumiak's keel of walrus ivory enables it to slide easily over the snow

Right below: Our team aboard Vernon's oumiak

The oumiak came to a halt, and Ron Church, from the best possible angle, filmed the large brownish mass against which gleamed the two scimiter-shaped tusks. The female, however, was uneasy. She reared up on her slab of ice, groaned, and began pushing her calf toward the water. In short order, both mother and calf disappeared with a splash into the sea.

Other blocks of ice were occupied, and it was irresistibly tempting to film those of the walruses who seemed, at least for the moment, placid enough to allow this liberty.

Then the men sighted an animal who was undoubtedly the patriarch of the herd, perched alone on his own personal slab of ice. The oumiak touched the slab, and Prezelin and Dorado leaped ashore, cameras in hand. The walrus appeared undisturbed by this invasion. The men advanced to within fifteen feet of him and remained there for at least thirty minutes, observing the animal and occasionally filming him. However, the resulting footage has the appearance of a series of still-life shots. The gestures of the old walrus, who would not condescend even to notice the cameramen, were very rare, and the scene is lacking in movement.

The walruses of the Bering Straits do not have the pinkish tint of their cousins on Round Island. If, as I suspect, the latter derive their color from exposure to the sun, then I can understand why the animals in the Bering

Straits are much darker than they, since there is nothing there but snow and fog. Their coats are, in fact, a reddish brown, and rather short; somewhat lighter than the coats of the Kodiak bears we had seen.

Finally, Dorado and Prezelin abandoned their attempt to enlist the cooperation of the patriarch. He was a hopelessly bad actor. They returned to the oumiak, and as they climed aboard, Vernon pointed out another mother and calf swimming a short distance away between the islands of a bank of ice. The mother walrus, however, was not in a mood to be filmed. She allowed the oumiak to approach close enough for the divers to work the cameras for a few minutes, then she launched a violent attack on the boat. Prezelin, who was at the rudder, succeeded in maneuvering so as to avoid the charge. But, as the walrus circled for another try, it occurred to him that the animal's battering ram of a head, armed with daggerlike tusks, could make short work indeed of the fragile oumiak. It was, after all, no more than a few thin sticks covered with walrus hide. He watched as the new attack was mounted and the massive head drew rapidly nearer, tusks glistening.

When the walrus was within a few feet of the oumiak, a shot rang out, and her body passed under the boat, striking its keel but without causing damage to the covering of hide. Vernon was grinning broadly, happy at this unexpected bounty. Fortunately, his aim was as good as his humor, and he had struck the attacking walrus squarely in the chest. Otherwise, our men would have had little chance for survival in the icy water, forty miles from Gambell.

The Eskimos have developed a technique for survival in such circumstances. They climb onto any block of ice floating nearby and haul their boat up after them. Then, they repair the boat. If, on the other hand, the boat has been sunk, their only chance of escape is to find an iceberg and remain on it either until it floats to shore or until they are lucky enough to be spotted by other Eskimo boats.

If our team had needed any proof of the necessity of experience and knowledge, Vernon himself would have been enough to convince them. He had killed the walrus, and then dragged its massive body onto the ice. There, he had cut it open with his razor-sharp knife, removed the hide and the tusks, carved large cuts of meat, and removed the stomach and the intestines. The whole operation lasted hardly more than two hours. No one but an Eskimo could have done it so quickly and so deftly. He worked the whole time without gloves, in the freezing cold, but he did not seem hurried. All the pieces of walrus were neatly stacked on the ice, then carefully loaded into the oumiak. There were probably over three hundred pounds of it by the time he had finished the job.

Ron Church, Prezelin, and Dorado had watched Vernon in fascination, oblivious to all else. By the time they returned to the boat, the dense fog had increased. The return trip to Gambell was difficult in the dim light of the polar night. It was past midnight when they arrived home.

Ron Church's team first used ordinary diving equipment with tanks of compressed air. But they were also eager to experiment in the cold water with our closed-circuit oxygen equipment. As soon as the oxygen tanks arrived by air, they made use of them in filming the walruses who were now in the waters around Gambell. This new equipment has the advantage of being relatively quiet in the water. The diver's breath does not form a stream of bubbles which rise toward the surface and often frighten marine animals; the men, therefore, were able to come quite close to the walruses. The oxygen apparatus is also lighter and easier to transport by oumiak, than tanks of compressed air. Finally, it offers a supplementary advantage. Since the diver breathes oxygen enclosed in a continuous circuit, the gas is able to warm to the temperature of the diver's lungs, and it is much less cold than compressed air.

There is, however, a major disadvantage. With the closed-circuit oxygen equipment, a diver cannot go deeper than twenty-five or thirty feet without risking a serious accident: loss of consciousness, nausea, and so forth.

Church, Prezelin, and Dorado made two dives with this new equipment, and their experiments provided useful data. We already knew the advantages and disadvantages under normal conditions, since we had often used the oxygen gear in observing sea otters, sea lions, and octopuses, but we had never before used it in polar waters.

The problems of the divers came not from their diving equipment but from their cameras. The cold arctic water presents numerous hazards for the filmmaker: condensation forms on equipment, and especially between the lens and the filter, and there is corrosion on all the internal elements of the cameras. The most difficult operation, however, was to change the film. In order to do so, the camera had to be taken back to Gambell after each shooting session, then heated for three or four hours. Only then could it be opened without danger of condensation. But, if the camera was loaded inside a house, condensation immediately formed on all its parts; and when the camera was taken outside, this moisture was transformed into ice. The team's first experiments in this respect ended in disaster. Eventually, they devised a workable solution, which consisted in leaving the camera outside permanently, and taking inside only the magazine wrapped in a plastic bag.

For thousands of years, the Eskimos of St. Lawrence Island have regarded the spring migration of walruses as their means of salvation. Until recently, their ice-covered rock was a place of hunger, as were all of the polar

regions. In this area, man has always existed precariously on the fringes of survival. It is this situation which has given the Eskimo his appetite for life, his talent as a hunter, and his store of courage. Nowadays, it is true, Gambell receives supplies by air, from the mainland. But there are still many of the 70,000 Eskimos living in the Arctic who owe, or will owe, their lives to providence in the form of a walrus or a bear.

Since the chief preoccupation of man in the Arctic is food, the passage of walruses in migration is the occasion of the year, and the walrus hunt is the event of the year. It is a festival, and one which coincides with another festival: the beginning of spring.

The walrus migration generally takes place between May 10 and May 30. Sometimes it takes place at night, as was the case in 1970 when a veritable fleet of swimming animals appeared suddenly in such numbers as to block the straits.

The hunt goes on until the first week of June. However, by then, the game is no longer the migrating walrus but the great herds of seals which arrive then and also provide the Eskimos with food and clothing.

The total walrus population of the Arctic is not very large. After being hunted for the past two hundred years, the number of them has fallen from

For many centuries, the Eskimos of Gambell were entirely dependent for their lives upon the migration of the walruses. In two centuries, the number of walruses in the herd has declined from 500,000 to 70,000. Between 10,000 and 12,000 animals are killed annually.

500,000 to no more than 70,000. Yet, the species is effectively protected by international legislation, and it is no longer — as it once was — in danger of extinction. A certain biological equilibrium has been established between the Eskimos on the one hand and the walruses on the other. In principle, there is no regulation governing the number of walruses that may be killed for their fat, their meat, or their hides, since the walrus is indispensable to the survival of the Eskimos. In practice, however, the citizens of St. Lawrence Island have established the maximum number of animals that may be killed each season: four per boat.

Between 10,000 and 12,000 walruses are killed every year by the inhabitants of Alaska and Siberia in order to provide them with the necessities of life. In addition, however, there is now a new toll taken annually, in the form of 3,500 more animals killed by trophy hunters. If that number should increase appreciably, then the fate of the walrus as a species would once more be in question — simply so as to satisfy the vanity of wealthy tourists. Even the latter, however, are subject to certain restrictions. They may kill only male walruses, and they must pay a fee of $100 for every animal they kill. Moreover, they are required to hire a professional guide, which provides the local Eskimos with a fair source of revenue.

The large, older male walruses are not considered dangerous. The younger males, however, are very aggressive, and they attack boats and humans without provocation. For this reason, they are the most feared by the Eskimos. Mother walruses with calves are also regarded as dangerous. In 1970, a half-dozen boats from Gambell were attacked by irritated mothers.

The time was when walrus attacks caused many deaths. Nowadays, the Eskimos have rifles and are experts in their use. They usually require only one shot to stop a charging walrus, as Vernon proved, thereby saving our men from a cold, and perhaps fatal, bath in the Arctic.

Although there is some doubt, as I have mentioned, that the walrus uses its tusks to dig for food on the bottom of the sea, there is none at all that it uses them very effectively as weapons at the surface. The tusks also serve as ice axes, and the walruses make good use of them in that capacity to climb out of the water onto a piece of ice which is sometimes rather high above the surface. We have seen them plant their tusks into the ice and hoist themselves up, with the help of their lower flippers, until they were lying on the ice.

It happened not infrequently that we photographed walruses with only a single tusk, or with two tusks one of which was broken. It seems likely that such deformations are caused by collisions with the ice rather than by combat. On this point, however, as on so many others concerning the walrus, our information is incomplete.

Our team prepares for an unpleasant experience: a dive beneath the ice

An Eskimo hunter fires at a walrus. The Eskimos now make use of modern weapons

Nine

The Happy Eskimo

From the airplane in which Philippe and I and the rest of the team made the trip to St. Lawrence, we could see groups of walruses pressed against one another on the floating ice as we flew over the Bering Sea.

The walruses had begun their migration. They were en route, and the blocks of ice, moving in a swift current, were carrying them northward. Thousands of young males and females were returning, as they did every spring, toward the glacial arctic seas where they would find the abundance of food required by their massive bodies.

Walruses, as I have said, are not remarkable swimmers. But they have compensating advantages. They are insensitive to the wind and the snow. The thick coat of fat which envelops them to a depth of five or six inches makes them immune to the cold. And, since they are unwilling to undertake the arduous swim northward, they manage to find floating blocks of ice going in the desired direction, like vagrants hitching rides on boxcars.

On these slabs, they travel either singly or in couples, for the male walruses, unlike elephant seals and seals, have no harems. They are monogamous by nature. When they are young, they are social animals and live in herds, but, later, the herds scatter and the individuals form smaller family groups.

The framework of this oumiak will be covered with the hides of female walruses

Left: The hunting of female walruses by the Eskimos results in many young walruses being orphaned and abandoned on the ice floes

Snow scooters have replaced dog sleds among the Eskimos of Gambell

The ice train of the walruses moves past St. Lawrence Island as it has for thousands of years; and, as they have for thousands of years, the Eskimos await the passage with great eagerness. For, despite the heavy toll taken by hunters and whalers over the centuries, the walrus remains the undoubted monarch of this country of storms and ice. There is an old Nordic refrain which came into my mind as I watched the stately procession of the walruses from the air:

Did you ever see a walrus smile,
All these many years?
Yes, I have seen a walrus smile,
But t'was hidden by his tears.

The only safeguards of the walrus in its tribulations have been those provided by nature: the hostility of the climate and the solitude of the frozen wastes.

As we flew over the snowy desert it occurred to me that down there, under the wings of our plane, the females were no doubt giving birth. The walruses carry their young for a year and then bear a single calf. No one has ever seen a walrus in the act of giving birth. Since the walruses are sheltered from killer whales and polar bears, and are now protected from man, this is sufficient to maintain the walrus population at a more or less stable level.

Our knowledge of the way walruses live in the wild is vague and incomplete. The frequent storms, and the unpredictable movement of the ice and the fog, make it difficult to observe them over an extended period of time. Entire herds of the animal may pass without being sighted. For the walrus has adapted so well to aquatic life that it can drift comfortably in the midst of the worst arctic storms, carried safely by the undertow through the most dangerous reefs and ice formations.

A Celebration

The Eskimo village of Gambell is a tiny human enclave, perched precariously on an island of ice and rock and wholly exposed to the elements. We had been looking forward to our arrival. But, when we landed, the cold and the dim light of the arctic sun left us somewhat disoriented. We all felt that we were far indeed from our sun-drenched home port of Monaco.

At the same time, we were fascinated by the snow and the ice, and we were eager to try the new diving suits of double thickness, which had been designed specially for this mission.

Work, however, had to wait. Our arrival at Gambell had been something of an event, and the Eskimos gave a feast in our honor. There was a dance, to the sound of the only musical instrument known to the Eskimos: a drum made from the stomach of a walrus. I quickly concluded that there was not a single part of the walrus for which the Eskimos had not found a practical use.

An Eskimo celebration at Gambell is not yet, thank goodness, a tourist attraction. The dances are not performed by a *corps de ballet* and organized by a corporation. Instead, the men and women of the village, wearing their festival costumes, moved about more or less haphazardly. They were obviously happy at the opportunity to don their beautiful, colorfully embroidered jackets, their loose pants of walrus hide, and their furred boots. Some of the young women, despite the heavily quilted silhouettes which they presented, were quite attractive, and the smiles on their round faces were charming.

Then, suddenly, the crowd of dancers scattered, and only two or three individuals remained on the floor. The others gathered around them, in a circle, and a dance began which I suspect is as old as the Eskimo. It consisted in a pantomime of all the animals and birds which have enabled the Eskimo to survive in their inhospitable country. The individual animals are evoked by means of simple, eloquent gestures, and the whole history of the relationship of man and animal is recounted with becoming gravity. It is less an entertainment than an act of homage and of thanksgiving.

Gravity, however, is not a sentiment which the Eskimos are able to sustain for very long. Someone made a joke, everyone laughed, tobacco was passed around, and the merrymaking began again.

Civilization

Except for the use of airplanes to communicate with the mainland, and of rifles in hunting, the life of the Eskimos has barely changed in the past two or three thousand years. They continue to hunt walruses, seals, whales, and birds for food and also in order to obtain the other necessities of life. Their clothing of sealskin — parkas, pants, and boots — are infinitely more effective against the cold than the best designed cold-weather gear available in Europe or the continental United States.

During the hunting season, food is set aside for winter. Meat is preserved in "freezers," which are holes dug in the ground and covered with ice. Even when the ocean freezes, however, the Eskimo is able to find food. He hunts foxes and wolves and even catches fish by cutting holes in the ice.

The body of a walrus which the Eskimos have just skinned

Despite the hardness of their lives, the Eskimos are a cheerful, happy people, and an engaging one. No matter how trying the circumstances, they lose neither their coolness nor their courage. They do not fear death, for their religious beliefs have persuaded them that death, far from being an object of fear, is a means of attaining a different and better life.

It is difficult for the outsider to understand why small groups of people persist, even today, in living in the Arctic. There are the Eskimos who are hunters and the Lapps who are animal herders. The answer, in both cases,

The distribution of walrus meat in Gambell takes place on the beach

The walrus's entrails are carefully dried, since the Eskimos make use of every part of the slain animal

The hides of the walruses are stretched out on frames so that they may be worked

may be found in the fact that both peoples have arrived at an almost perfect solution to the problems posed by their environment. That solution is found in the equilibrium which has been established among men, animals, and climate. Such natural equilibrium is one of the essential conditions of human happiness, yet it is a secret which we "civilized" men seem to have forgotten.

Man, it is true, has destroyed great numbers of animals. But there are certain species which have managed to survive in sufficient numbers to maintain the biological balance between the life-giving animal and the hunting humans. This is what occurred with respect to the walrus and the Eskimo. Even with his modern weapons, the Eskimos are content to kill only that number of animals which is necessary to their own survival.

This realistic approach to conservation was the occasion of a slight misunderstanding upon our arrival at Gambell. At that time, there was a bill before the Congress of the United States which would have declared all marine mammals to be totally protected species. The Eskimos were afraid that our film would move public opinion in favor of the walruses and that they would no longer be allowed to hunt these animals.

We did what we could to reassure them. Certainly, I am in favor of the most stringent protection of certain species of marine mammals. At the same time, we must recall that the civilization of the Eskimos is, in effect, a walrus civilization. To outlaw the hunting of walruses would be to destroy a human, economic, and ecological balance which has survived intact for millennia. This is the message which we tried to convey in the film shot on St. Lawrence Island.

By a curious paradox, the walrus is now in danger but not from the Eskimo. It is in danger from us Occidentals. For a long time, the annual migration of the walruses allowed these animals to find refuge in glacial waters which were inaccessible to man. Now, however, the airplane and the facilities of civilization have moved into the polar seas, and hunters from the West are able to invade the Far North in search of "trophies" to exhibit to their friends. The polar safari, in fact, has become quite fashionable. It is perhaps the least justifiable of all safaris and it is this abuse, far more than the walrus hunt of the Eskimos, which endangers the species.

Eskimo Life

Physically, the Eskimo has an Asiatic appearance, with a flat face and oriental features. A large number of Eskimos wear glasses. Their myopia is perhaps the result of poor diet or it may be the consequence of the constant glare to which their ancestors were subjected by the combination of light and snow. Some of the older women still have the traditional Eskimo tattoos on their faces.

A number of the Eskimos at Gambell are employed by the government, especially as postmen and teachers. Others support themselves by hunting. And some live from the tourist trade and act as guides or carve ivory to sell to visitors.

At Gambell, there are several buildings of masonry, all built by the government, such as the school and the hospital. Most of the houses are of wood and are quite comfortable. Then, finally, there are the shacks, many of them in sorry condition.

Our friends Prezelin and Dorado noted several changes which had taken place since their visit two years earlier. A kind of supermarket had been built and was doing a land-office business, since the Eskimos are openhanded spenders. Some of the houses were now equipped with running water. However, there was still a public well in the center of the village. This well remains open all year. It does not freeze because a heating system has been installed in it, near the surface of the water.

The most important recent improvement consists in a generator which supplies electricity to the houses and illuminates the village's only street during the arctic night.

The Dog Problem

The multiplication of machines has not only affected the lives of the Eskimos but has also destroyed forever the silence of the Far North. Noisy snowmobiles, belching fumes, are very popular with both men and women. From morning till night, Gambell resounds with the noise of engines and the blare of horns. Usually, a snowmobile lasts for only one season. As soon as the ice melts, the vehicle is abandoned where it stands. When winter comes again, it is useless. Indeed, often it cannot be found under the snow.

Another vehicle has now appeared in Gambell and has contributed to the noisy traffic of this tiny village. This is the snowcart, or snow tiger, which is larger and more powerful than the snowmobile. It is in fact a small snow truck equipped with six balloon tires and six small wheels mounted on three axles. There are two seats in the front section of this machine and an enclosed space in the rear where one may carry a seal, or barrels of fat, or cans of fuel.

The introduction of motorized vehicles has resulted in the almost total disappearance of that traditional symbol of Eskimo civilization, the dog sled.

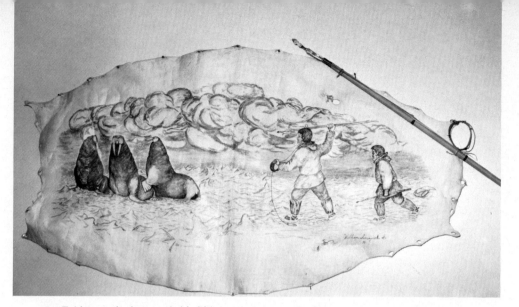

An Eskimo artist has used this hide as a canvas to depict a scene from a seal hunt

At Gambell, for instance, there is only one sled in use. Curiously, its owner is European, the Protestant missionary. From time to time, he hitches up his dogs and takes a solitary, nostalgic ride around the village, for the sake of tradition. The Eskimos, on the other hand, are not concerned about tradition. To their mind, the dog sled is an outdated means of transport, on a par with the horse and buggy of the white man.

A sad consequence of the abandonment of the sled is the situation of the dogs, those beautiful, thick-furred huskies whose courage and endurance were once legendary in the North. They have been more or less abandoned, and their lot is not happy. They wander around the village. Most of them are hardly ever fed, and they must dig in the garbage for food. Still, the Eskimos have never been able to make up their minds to give up their dogs altogether and allow them to die of hunger. They keep their favorites tied up outside their houses and feed them regularly. But huskies were not made to spend their lives at the end of a short rope. They were made for long treks across the snow, for running, and, occasionally, for fighting. One of our few melancholy memories of Gambell is that of dogs, howling in sadness and boredom.

The Consumer Society

Eskimos, as though determined to prove that they are truly civilized, now dress as everyone else does. They buy fur-lined coats and no longer wear their embroidered parkas except on festive occasions. One of their most important forms of entertainment consists in studying the mail-order catalogues and ordering the items that strike their fancy. The idea of selling refrigerators to

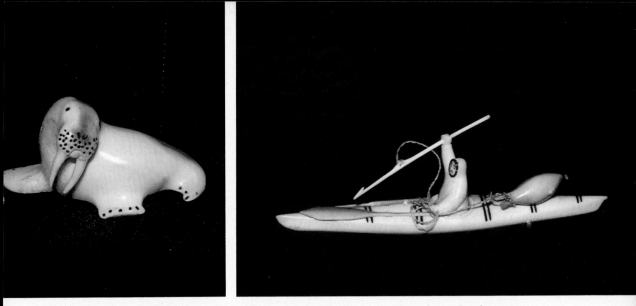

Carving and engraving are traditional arts among the Eskimos. These ivory figurines are intended for sale to tourists

Eskimos is no longer a joke. They order these machines through their catalogues and, when the refrigerators arrive, they are proudly installed in the Eskimos' houses. Obviously, they are not needed for refrigeration. They are used as pantries.

It is an occasion when a citizen of Gambell receives a package in the mail. It is hurriedly unwrapped in the snowy street, as the recipient's friends and neighbors cluster around to see what it contains. And, naturally, everyone must immediately try the new acquisition, whether it be a coat or a snowmobile or a rifle.

An Eskimo engraver lives in relative comfort. Such skills are among the major resources of the modern Eskimo community

The Eskimos have developed a great affection for firearms. When a hunting party of five or six Eskimos goes out in an oumiak, each man usually has three or four rifles with him, and the shells are all over the boat. One of the guides who accompanied us, in addition to his rifles, had a pistol strapped to each hip.

Eskimos, generally speaking, are good shots. However, they are trigger happy and shoot at anything merely for the joy of it. When a boy reaches the age of ten or twelve, he is given a rifle. He then proceeds to shoot at anything that moves, a practice which is not without a certain risk for strangers.

The outboard motors in common use on the oumiaks serve as status symbols as well as conveniences. As the Eskimos do not seem to have a knack for tinkering, they are unable to repair these engines or even to maintain them properly. Therefore, when a motor breaks down, it is simply abandoned. It goes without saying that the inoperative engine is always at fault.

The question arises of where the Eskimos find the money for such conspicuous consumption. In that respect, it should be noted that there is an excellent market for walrus skins. And Eskimo folk art, such as carved ivory, brings a good price from tourists. Moreover, all Eskimo communities receive subsidies from the American Government.

The most profitable occupation of the Eskimo is that of hunting guide to the many parties who come to kill walruses. The visiting hunter pays a hunting fee, then pays the Eskimo guide, as well as all expenses for supplies and equipment. The hunters are provided with room and board in the guide's home, for which he pays a hundred dollars per day and per outing.

The Eskimos save little of the money that passes through their hands. They are not a saving people, and they love to spend. They live from day to day, without much thought of what the morrow may bring. They are extremely hospitable and welcome all visitors warmly and generously. For thousands of years, they have been accustomed to community life. Therefore, they have very little sense of personal possessions, and they are always short of cash.

Eskimo women have an agreeable appearance, although, by the standards of Western nations, they are not particularly beautiful. Their faces are marked with wrinkles early in life, probably because of the wind, the cold, and the glare of the sun on the ice. They are hard workers and excellent housekeepers and mothers, but they take no part in the hunt.

In Vernon's house, we lived on the second floor — the attic, really — while he and his wife and their children lived on the ground floor. There was a bathroom but no running water.

It is possible that the present life-style of the Eskimo, with its relative comfort and its contact wtih the West, will cause him gradually to lose the traditional virtues of his people and the skills of which his ancestors were past masters and which allowed them to survive in the Arctic.

Yet, even today, the Eskimos we saw remained very adept at carving a dead walrus. In no more than fifteen minutes, a team of two or three Eskimos can skin an animal. They know how to carve the meat of the walrus and precisely at what spot to make a cut. They remove only those parts and organs that they find useful. But when the hunt has been particularly good, they will sometimes leave the dead walruses almost intact. In such instances, they do not bother to carve all of the animals, but remove only the tusks.

Electricity, running water, and noisy snow vehicles have all turned Gambell into a "modern" village; but, side by side with these conveniences, the settlement has retained much of its Eskimo character. One has only to walk down the street and see the walrus hides, stretched out on wooden frames near the houses, to realize that the old ways are far from dead.

When the winds blow at a hundred miles an hour and drifts form against the houses, burying the snowmobiles and breaking the electric cables, nature triumphs over man's precarious civilization. Then, the Eskimos huddle in their houses, as their ancestors did, and venture out only for the shortest time possible, so as to conserve their energies. Meanwhile, their dogs, still tied outside, lie buried in the snow.

During the winter months, while the Eskimos remain in their houses, many of them occupy the time by carving ivory. Some of them are gifted sculptors and execute statues and carvings of walruses, of bear hunters, or of the grotesque masks which form part of their folk legends. The art of the Eskimos is ancient, and it is not without its masterpieces. They have been carvers and sculptors for thousands of years.

Since the American Government does not allow the export of raw ivory, walrus tusks must be carved or engraved before they may be shipped out of Alaska. This not only increases the value of the ivory but also provides work for the residents of the area. On St. Lawrence Island, during the winter, 90 per cent of the population is unemployed. Therefore, everyone has taken up sculpting and carving. The results are not always happy, for not all Eskimos are great artists. Some of them repeat the same design over and over again, planning to sell their work to tourists. It seems to me that this situation may well endanger the integrity of an original and authentic art form, one typical

Following page: A worthwhile, if uncomfortable, dive off Gambell, beyond the wall of ice blocks which lines the shore

of the Far North and symbolic of man's difficult life there. However, I have often wondered whether the Eskimos really believe in the hideous storm demons and ice devils which are the principal subjects of their art.

I visited a sculptor during our stay on St. Lawrence. He worked sitting on the floor, in a cluttered room, surrounded by puppies. As he carved, his wife plied her needle on a waterproof coat, using strips of walrus gut as thread. Her smiling, sensitive face was heavily tattooed. She said that the tattoos dated from the time of her marriage. The custom had now passed, she explained, and the younger women refused to allow themselves to be so decorated.

The sculptor also smiled and sang as he worked. He had a sly air about him, which is not uncommon among Eskimos, but this did not prevent him from showing himself both hospitable and generous.

I had been told that the artists of Gambell were in the habit of singing folk songs as they worked. As I listened to the lyrics of my host, I realized that his refrain came not from the past but more likely from the office of a publicity agent. It went something like this:

Carve, carve!
For our customers in San Francisco,
For those in Oklahoma,
And even in Mexico,
Topeka, Topeka,
And also in Alaska.

As he sang, his wife occasionally left her sewing to perform a little dance, which was nothing more than a few movements accompanied by hand gestures.

The scene was naive, perhaps, even childlike, but by no means ridiculous. Obviously, this couple — who, twenty years before, had not hesitated to brave the ice and the snow with a dog sled — had now transformed themselves into a commercial and touristic enterprise, from which they derived most of their income. Even in the Arctic, one must live.

A Good Omen

When we first arrived at Gambell, the Eskimos had killed a whale, and the entire village was busy carving it up. The oldest hunters of the village supervised the work and gave instructions regarding the distribution of the pieces among the families of Gambell.

It was a good omen, for the great body of the whale was sufficient to provide meat and blubber for everyone in the area. Moreover, the mammal's body was regarded as the property of everyone, for everyone had contributed to its acquisition. Several hunters had killed it with rifles, then it had been towed to shore — a task which required the services of every oumiak in Gambell.

The Eskimos have a highly developed sense of community solidarity. As a group, they "stick together" — even though, as individuals, they often argue and disagree. Moreover, all the families in Gambell are divided into three clans, among which peace does not always reign.

The old men of the village, the "village fathers," station themselves on the beach, where they keep more or less permanent watch. Their function is important, and sometimes saves lives. They know which oumiaks have gone out to sea, how long they have been gone, which of them have returned, and which are still out. They study changes in the weather and variations in the wind, and they observe the passing of herds of walruses and seals. They give the alarm when necessary and decide when a search or rescue party should be sent out. These elders — all of them between sixty and eighty years of age — seem sure of foot and eye. In return for the services they render, they have a right to pieces of walrus when the oumiaks return to shore.

Despite the comforts provided by the advent of civilization, the Eskimos still live difficult lives. The ice, the cold, and the storms remain fearsome enemies. Hunting and fishing do not always provide sufficient food. Still, they love their homeland, hostile as it seems; and the larger cities of Alaska, where they could lead more comfortable lives, hold no attraction for the middle-aged and older residents of the village. The young people are sent to school on the mainland, and when they return, they are often dissatisfied with their village and sometimes have acquired the habit of using drugs.

Until the ages of ten to twelve years, the scholastic aptitude of young Eskimos is at least equal to that of Western children of the same age. Later, however, the Eskimos seem to have difficulty pursuing studies at the university level. The explanation, it seems, is that their intelligence, acute as it is, is not at home with abstractions. The orientation of the Eskimo is wholly toward the realm of the practical.

It is to be feared, as I have already mentioned, that the new generation is in the process of forgetting the traditional skills which have permitted their people to survive in the murderous climate: hunting, fishing, the fabrication of warm clothing, survival in the arctic wilderness, and especially navigation among slabs of ice in a stormy sea. Even now, in Gambell, there is only one person, an old woman, who is skilled enough to be able to slice walrus hide to the proper thickness for an oumiak.

The oumiak is itself a work of art, a marvelous tool which enables man to venture out into ice-covered seas in which our zodiacs and launches would be crushed in short order. It is a narrow boat, pointed at both ends, capable of maneuvering through the narrowest openings. Its frame is of wood, like that of a kayak, but it is very flexible and virtually unbreakable. The hull of the oumiak is made of the hides of female walruses, for the reason that the females' hides do not have the wounds (or holes) that the males inflict on one another in combat.

The oumiak is light enought to be carried over the ice; moreover, its keel is covered with pieces of ivory from walrus tusks, so that it slides easily over snow of any consistency.

It is a craft which sits fairly high, and its planking rises to about three feet above the surface. There is a secret in the manufacture of a proper oumiak, and perhaps a touch of magic, which consists in fitting the boat together in a special way so that it does not shatter in a collision.

In the Sea

On St. Lawrence Island, a sunny day is a rare event. Even on such occasions, it is not the kind of sun that we are accustomed to in more temperate climates. The arctic sun is always slightly veiled, dimmed by the grayness of the sky. The days are long. In May, the sun sets at 11 P.M. and rises at 2 A.M. Even the short night is not really dark, for there is always a dim light over the sea.

The ice banks around St. Lawrence are a favorite sunning place for seals, and these animals are more common in the area than walruses. These are bearded, black-eyed seals, with reddish-brown coats and whiskers like a brush. They average about eight feet in length and reach a weight of over five hundred pounds. They dig for food on the sea bottom, but they have no tusks for that purpose. Instead, they use their square flippers as digging tools. They spend almost the entire year near the shore and are valued as game by the Eskimos.

The walruses, on the other hand, are usually at a distance from St. Lawrence. We have wandered over the sea for as long as twenty-two hours at a stretch without sighting them. One day when we finally decided to turn back to Gambell, the fog had become so thick that we could barely see the prow of our boat, and we could not get our bearings. It was not until 5 A.M. that we reached the village, frozen to the bone and so tired that we could hardly move.

Vernon Slwooko watches skeptically as François Dorado prepares to build an igloo

The igloo begins to take shape

We wanted, at least once, to cut a hole through the floe and dive beneath the ice. The team we sent down — Philippe, Bonnici, Giacoletto, and Dorado — had a difficult time of it. They found themselves becoming increasingly uneasy as they went down toward the bottom, apprehensive about their ability to find the opening in the ice. They looked upward constantly to make certain that the hole was still open.

The water was cloudy with plankton, and the ice on the surface was so thick that hardly any light shone through it. A strong current carried the divers under the icy vault on the surface, and it goes without saying that there was no chance of spotting a walrus, or even a seal. There were, however, numerous empty shells.

All in all, it was a very difficult and unrewarding dive. It can be fairly said that it was one of the most arduous dives ever undertaken by *Calypso*'s men.

Strangely enough, there has been very little written about the sensations experienced under conditions of intense cold. It seems that man, who has a whole series of adjectives to describe heat, is at a loss when he must put into words what happens when he suffers from cold. The reason, perhaps, is that man's past has been spent in temperate regions; or it may be that intense cold, unlike intense heat, numbs the mind so that it is unable to analyze the nuances of pain to which the body is subjected.

Immersion in the water of the Arctic first of all gives the sensation of being pricked simultaneously by thousands of sharp needles. One feels a stiffness throughout one's body, and a metal-like hardness. It is as though all of one's limbs had been suddenly turned not into lead but into steel. The chill seems to penetrate the marrow of one's spine and into the vertebrae, like a sharp surgical instrument. One's back seems to draw back before the torment of the cold, before that presence of pain which is the enemy of life. It is all that one can do not to scream in terror.

Our divers went down to a hundred feet. In their ascent, they saw the bubbles from their breathing apparatus imprisoned under the ice over their heads. When they emerged from the hole, their sense of relief was intense. Even then, however, there was danger. The blocks of ice on the floe are balanced very precariously, and at any moment one of them may come crashing down upon someone, or else seal up the hole in the floe.

Among the divers who went down, Philippe suffered the least. Bonnici's hands were paralyzed, and he was so swollen that he could barely move. Dorado's face was puffed up like a balloon.

We now understand why it is that Eskimos never swim.

The bad weather continued unabated. We went out on the water, but the gray, cloud-laden sky made it difficult for us to get good footage. While waiting for a better light, it occurred to us that we might be able to film, on land, the building of an igloo — a shelter constructed entirely of blocks of ice. As uncomfortable at it may sound, the igloo has saved the lives of many Eskimo hunters obliged to spend the night in the open. Some Eskimos spend the entire winter in these shelters. The word *igloo* means simply "house."

When we communicated our plan to our friends in Gambell, we were astonished to learn that there was not a single resident of the village who knew how to go about constructing an igloo. Finally, one man was found who had once seen one built, and Prezelin and Dorado set to work, under his direction, cutting blocks of ice with a handsaw. As it turned out, the man had long since forgotten whatever he might have once known about igloos, and Prezelin and Dorado's hard work was all for nothing. However, it did provide free entertainment for the Eskimos who gathered around to watch us at work. They seemed vastly amused at the idea that a group of Frenchmen would want to build an igloo.

At this point, it seems superfluous to remark that, contrary to popular belief, not all Eskimos live in igloos. Only the Eskimos of the Canadian Arctic make use of this traditional kind of shelter. It is possible that Eskimos who move about on the floes are able, in a short time, to throw together a shelter of some kind out of ice and snow. But no one in Gambell had ever had occasion to do so. They preferred building their houses out of the bones of whales and walruses.

We happened one day upon an abandoned village where the foundations of the houses were of stone and the walls of whale vertebrae. Some of these bones weighed over two hundred pounds, and since the village was situated two miles from the sea, we could only assume that the builders had carried them that distance. It was no doubt a very old village, evidence of an ancient Eskimo settlement, for Prezelin and Dorado found some arrowheads of stone.

Upon our return to Gambell, we spoke to some of the elders about this abandoned village. They seemed quite upset that we had visited the place and begged us not to return, saying that we must not disturb these vestiges of the past which they held in reverence. It goes without saying that we did as they asked.

There is much discussion of the origin of Eskimos, but very little is known for certain. We can say only that they are the descendants of a society of hunters and fishermen, who arrived in the arctic region approximately 10,000 years ago, and that their art and their religious beliefs are related to

Dorado and Prezelin move into their new house. Ironically, this was the only igloo built at Gambell

those of certain Siberian tribes.

Archaeological findings in northern Siberia, in the Chukchi Peninsula, indicate that the ancestors of the Eskimos came from islands in the South Seas and sailed along the eastern coast of Asia to Kamchatka. From there, it appears that they reached the Bering Straits. Rudenko, a Russian ethnographer, has pointed out the similarity of the ivory and bone carvings in the Bering Sea area to those on very old pottery found in Melanesia.* This theory would explain the abilities of the Eskimos as seamen, boatbuilders, harpooners, and exceptional hunters of marine mammals — all talents necessary to survival in a land of ice.

*One of the major groupings of Pacific Ocean islands, northeast of Australia.

Until very recently, the Eskimos constituted one of the last surviving hunter societies and one of the last truly communal societies on the face of the earth. Even today, an Eskimo's personal possessions are limited to his weapons, his tools, his oumiak, and his kayak. The ownership of land means nothing to him, and since he is not a herder, like the Lapps, he is not interested in owning animals. The resources of nature, to the Eskimo, are the property of all men, and he shares them as willingly with strangers as with friends. On the other hand, if an Eskimo becomes ill, or is injured, the entire community can be counted upon to come to his aid.

The aim of the Eskimo has never been to become wealthy. It has been to develop his skills, to become more and more proficient at hunting and fishing, in the making of clothing, weapons, traps, and boats. These were all tenets of the law of survival as articulated in the Far North.

Now, this view of life has been shaken by the advent of modern civilization; and it will be shaken even more severely in the future, not only in its physical aspects, but, more important, in its moral principles. Brought face to face with the consumer society, the Eskimo has begun to learn the value of money and to acquire a taste for personal possessions. However, it is not impossible that the genius of the race may somehow find a way to safeguard its traditional Eskimo values. The homeland of the Eskimo is a vast treasury of natural wealth, and the Eskimo himself is amply equipped to take advantage of that wealth, to attain a higher standard of living, and, simultaneously, to remain an Eskimo.

Walruses riding their islands of ice

Preparations for departure in the oumiak

Ten

Springtime in the Arctic

Almost all of our divers are natives of the South of France. The waters to which they are accustomed are those of the Mediterranean, the Red Sea, and the Caribbean. It is no wonder that the icy water of the Arctic, the lowering sky, and the constant fog had a depressing effect upon them. Yet, their morale remained at its customary high level, and they bore up admirably under the hardships imposed upon them by the intemperate climate. The only hint of their Mediterranean origin occurred when the sun occasionally burst forth, and then their delight and their relief was double that of anyone else's. The rays of the sun seemed to revitalize them.

There was one such period during our stay at Gambell: five glorious, windless days of bright sunlight. Most of the year, the weather is unbelievably foul, interrupted only by a spell of sunshine of more or less brief duration, a mere interruption of the storms. In such circumstances, fine weather seems all the more precious because of its rarity.

On this occasion, there were thousands of birds circling against the blue sky, and the plain of ice around Gambell glistened dimly, like a skating rink. The sky was so clear that we finally glimpsed the mountains on the horizon, still white but punctuated here and there by black rocks announcing that the spring thaw had, in fact, begun.

The sea was like a lovely blue-green lake, moving gently against the melting blocks of ice which lined the shore. It was a scene of magical beauty, suddenly conjured up out of the grayness and fog and snow of the previous day. The icebergs were tinged with dark blue and emerald green, and the melting snow glittered with touches of gold. Here, more than elsewhere, the coming of spring awakens and illuminates the world with the soft, muted arctic light emanating in pastel rays from an orange sun visible both night and day. At midday, however, the glare from the plain of snow is painful to the eyes, and there are gusts of heat on one's skin. Finally, the winter is over. Finally, a man can touch a metal object without leaving a piece of skin on it. Finally, the air no longer chills one's lungs.

The five days of unexpected grace represented a great opportunity for us, and we were quick to take advantage of it. We spent the whole time shooting our walrus film. Early the first morning, we gathered up our cameras and diving gear and set out across the ice with Vernon's oumiak. It seemed strange. We were accustomed to the convenience of *Calypso,* to zodiacs and launches and diving saucers — none of which would have been even remotely useful here. They would have been crushed by the ice in short order. Instead, we were carrying an oumiak, a primitive, archaic handmade craft of fragile appearance which, nonetheless, can withstand almost any impact and which, because it is so light, can go virtually anywhere. It is the product of long experience, a tool painstakingly elaborated by man and perfectly adapted to its specialized function.

Getting the oumiak to the open water was not as easy as it might sound. The ice, broken up by the swell during the night, was piled up like giant cubes of sugar — except that the cubes were in constant motion, crashing against one another, then separating occasionally to reveal a stretch of black water. In order to keep our footing, we relied upon a pick and upon our agility in jumping from one block of ice to another and, somehow, not slipping into the water in the process. There were moments when it seemed we would never make it. But Vernon was imperturbable in the midst of this chaos. With the help of our team, which had now had some experience on the ice, he deftly moved his boat toward the water, from one block to the next, through the ruins of the floe.

Vernon seemed somehow to know precisely where we would find an ice-free channel to the open water, and he went to it directly and unerringly. Finally, we dropped the oumiak into the water and climbed aboard. But the end was not yet. There were still blocks of ice to be skirted in the water, or to be pushed aside if they were small enough, as we made our way painfully forward.

The weather took a turn for the better, and the ice began to melt. But it was still cold at Gambell

Our guide kept his eyes ahead, computing the course we would follow. He found a narrow, ice-edged channel, which looked promising, and signaled Prezelin to start up the outboard motor.

The motor's purr broke the arctic silence as we zigzagged carefully from one passage to another. Behind us, the small cluster of Gambell's houses, dominated by the village's radio antenna, faded into the distance and became part of the universal whiteness.

Vernon was our navigator. From his place on the bow, he signaled to Bonnici to slow down or to speed up as he picked his way between the floes by distinguishing the colors of the hard ice from those of the melting blocks. Thus, warmed by the sun, we allowed ourselves to be carried in the oumiak through a world which was neither liquid nor solid but blindingly white and crystalline in the raw light.

The oumiak skirted icebergs which seemed ready to tumble down upon us. Occasionally, the walrus-hide skin of the boat brushed alarmingly against a submerged ice formation. In the most difficult places, Vernon used a boathook to push the oumiak free, or else planted his *tok,* or pick, into the piece of ice and used it as a pivot on which we moved around the obstruction. On several occasions, when it seemed certain that we would be crushed between two blocks of ice, Vernon leaped out of the oumiak onto one of them and pushed away the other with his feet so that we could get through.

This was the first clear day on which we had been on the water, and we were now able to appreciate the great number of icebergs floating gently around St. Lawrence Island. They were of all sizes and shapes, and some of them were remarkable. Despite the difficulties they presented to navigation, we could not help but admire these drifting, glistening castles of ice. In their depths, the ice had the deep blueness of the rarest diamonds. Some of them were riddled with caves and tunnels. Some, as they passed, loosed sheets of ice into the water with a mighty splash. And from some of them, snow cascaded down in miniature avalanches.

Before us now was the open water, broken only by occasional formations of ice. We scanned the floating islands for walruses but without success. The oumiak continued on, leaving a long wake in the still water. I looked around and saw nothing. The sky and the sea blended together at the horizon into a single substance. Then, when we were about eighteen miles off the Siberian coast, Vernon pointed to something in the distance. His eyes are as keen in the sunlight as in the fog, for it was several seconds before we were able to see them: the black dots which marked the presence of walruses. As we drew nearer, we could see that the animals were asleep, blissful in the warmth of spring. There were two groups of them. Five were stretched out on one island, ten on another.

Vernon maneuvered expertly so as to approach the animals with the wind. Their eyesight is effective at a distance of only twenty or thirty yards.

The walruses remained motionless as we drew nearer. Like most marine mammals, they are rather lazy when on land. It also occurred to me that perhaps these animals had never before seen human beings. Then, when the oumiak touched the island, a large reddish-brown mass rose, tusks gleaming, to stare at us. The animal roared and its companions looked up lazily, then immediately fell asleep again.

A Movie Star

I climbed onto the ice, followed by Philippe carrying his camera. I crawled toward the group and saw that all five of the animals were of good size. The largest of them was the one who had spotted us as we landed. He was still alert, watching. The other four now awoke once more and began dragging themselves awkwardly toward the water. We heard a loud splash, and the floating piece of ice on which we crouched heaved in the water.

The large walrus had still not moved, and his eyes never left us. We froze where we were, afraid that, if we moved, this one would also escape into the sea. Both Philippe and I felt instinctively that this bold fellow would be a star of the first magnitude for our film.

The four walruses who had gone into the water remained near their napping place, their heads above the surface, watching to see what would happen on their island. Obviously, they were waiting for their companion and did not know quite what to make of all this.

On occasions like this one, it is very hard not to interpret an animal's attitude within the framework of human expectations. It occurred to me that the walruses in the water might be waiting to watch the battle which they expected to take place between us and the large walrus; or that they were perhaps afraid for the walrus who, from his size, might well be the leader of the group.

There was silence. Not even a groan from our walrus. Faintly, I heard a sound in the water. One of the four other walruses was swimming slowly toward the island. I could see his brushlike whiskers, his small, inexpressive eyes, his receding chin, his long tusks raised menacingly above the water. As he approached, I knew that, if he was of a mind to charge, Philippe and I would undoubtedly be tumbled into the water and probably be attacked there both by the newcomer and by the old patriarch.

But the walrus had not returned on our account. He moved toward the

larger animal, who was poised at the edge of the ice, and stopped before him.

I was quite near the pair, and Philippe had managed to get into a position where he could film the scene from a good angle. We were absolutely still. There was not a sound from our friends in the oumiak. We all held our breath and waited. The scene, an instance of free animals in unhampered contact, seemed extraordinary, almost miraculous.

The old walrus now lowered his head toward the other animal floating before him. The two heads touched, nostrils dilated. The extended whiskers of the two walruses came into contact.

What was happening? What did this contact signify? Once more, I was acutely aware of the wall of incomprehension which separates man and animal. And once more, I had recourse to anthropomorphism. If the two walruses were "talking" by touching heads and whiskers, what were they "saying"? Was the one in the water trying to persuade the other to leave the island to the intruders and take refuge in the sea where he would be invulnerable? Or were they formulating a plan of attack?

It was first necessary to get the oumiak to the beach; then we had to haul it over the barricade of ice blocks surrounding the island. These maneuvers sometimes resulted in an unexpected icy bath

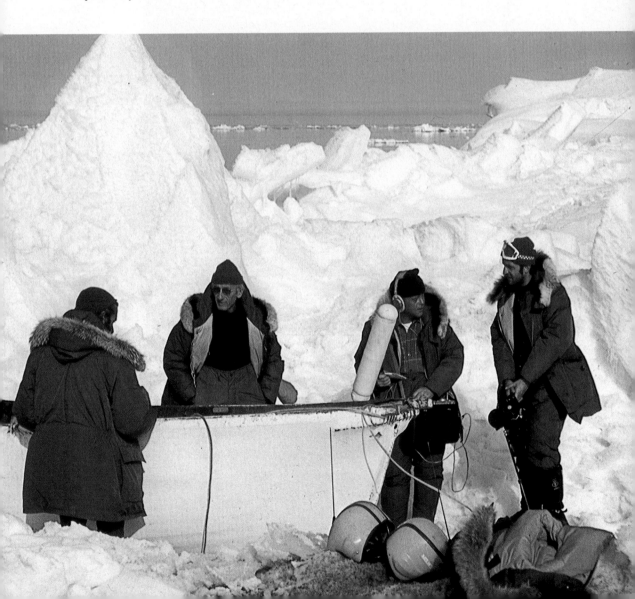

We watched, fascinated. The large walrus raised his head and looked at us. Then, the other swam away to rejoin the three walruses who had remained a short distance from the slab of ice. It may be that the walrus's mission had been of a diplomatic nature and that it failed because of the determination of the patriarch.

We know, in any event, that some exchange had taken place among the five animals — an exchange the meaning of which we were unable to decipher. How frustrating it is to be so much at a loss when we try to understand even the simplest aspects of animal behavior. In this instance, all we knew was that walruses exhibit a sense of solidarity with other walruses. The Eskimos have seen them help one another. When one animal is wounded, for instance, the others gather around him and often attack the hunter. This trait, unfortunately, is responsible for many a massacre. Usually, the walruses who come to the aid of their wounded companion are themselves killed.

Suddenly, the four walruses in the water began moving in a group, heads high and tusks at the ready, directly toward Vernon's oumiak. The Eskimo and our friends fled precipitously, outboard roaring, in inglorious retreat.

It is just as well that they chose not to contest the issue. The tactic of the walruses is to sink their tusks into the oumiak's covering of hide and to slash sideways. The four animals would have reduced the oumiak to shreds in a matter of seconds, and everyone would have ended up in the icy water.

The walruses, seeing that the victory was theirs, dived and disappeared, leaving the large walrus alone on his floating island.

There was nothing to prevent the oumiak from returning to the island. When it did so, I instructed our sound engineer to remain in the boat, and I took a radio microphone with me as I began crawling again toward the walrus. It may be that I was being overly careful, but I kept in mind that I was facing an animal weighing two or three thousand pounds and that walruses are not nearly as even-tempered as elephant seals. As Philippe's camera whirled, I pulled myself to within ten feet of the walrus. There was no noticeable reaction on his part. Then I rose until I was kneeling before him. This change in posture did not seem to please him. He reared up higher than before until his head was higher than mine. Then he struck at me, or at least in my direction, with his tusks. His posture was one of open hostility. I saw the massive head, the erect whiskers, the thick lips parted before the black cavity of his mouth. A long growl of exasperation rumbled from his throat.

I decided that this show of hostility was a mere tactic of intimidation, intended to frighten me away from the walrus's personal island and sun; and I adopted the same tactic. I got to my feet, and now I was taller than the walrus. Immediately, his demonstration came to a halt. Then, I quickly lay on my stomach, and he reared up. We repeated the game several times. Whenever I lay on the ground, the walrus pretended to be ready to attack.

Victory in the Cold War

Philippe was watching our antics, laughing. Finally, I tried something new. I jumped to my feet, waved my arms, and began shouting. This, apparently, was enough to win the game for me. The walrus, now thoroughly unhappy, dived into the sea. Before it struck the water, I clearly heard the sound of a bell. Dingdong. It was quite distinct. At first, I thought someone in the oumiak had switched on a transistor radio. I turned angrily and began, "What idiot—"

I stopped. The sound had not come from the direction of the boat but from the walrus. Vernon confirmed this. The walrus, I discovered, is able to make a bell-like sound consisting of two notes. It has two pharyngetic pockets in which it retains air from its lungs and by means of which it emits this extraordinary sound. We do not know its meaning or its purpose. It is said that it is heard more frequently during the mating season than at other times.

The behavior of the walrus, when I approached it, was less mysterious than the bell sounds, given the fact that walruses fight among themselves to defend their personal territories. These fights, however, consist mostly of attempts at intimidation, designed to frighten an adversary away from a particular piece of ice. The strength of the antagonists is measured by the length of their tusks and by the height of their heads above the ground. The weaker — that is, the smaller walrus with the shorter tusks — then acknowledges defeat and leaves. Actual combat, at least combat of a serious nature, takes place only between walruses of equal strength. Obviously, my old walrus would not condescend to fight me, since I was much smaller than he.

Despite the rarity of the bell sound I had heard at the end of our encounter, it turned out that walruses are quite talkative in the water. We lowered microphones into the sea and recorded an extraordinary concert of the cracking and clapping sounds which are characteristic of walruses in the water and which may be heard at a considerable distance.

While our tape machine was recording these sounds, Prezelin dived. He was able only to glimpse two walruses, while there were at least several dozen others scattered around the oumiak, "talking" among themselves.

Humpback whales also make sounds in the water, but these sounds are a form of singing. Those of the walruses are more like a cry which begins high and descends the scale. My hypothesis is that the walruses use this variable frequency as a modulating-frequency sonar device, which is the last word in

Finally, the sea was calm and the sky was clear. The oumiak wove its way through the floating chunks of ice, and, suddenly, we caught sight of several walruses on a floe

technology. This sonar device, I imagine, is used to locate obstacles in the water.

In any event, the cries of the walruses in the Bering Straits resound between the layer of ice on the surface and the flat bottom. They may be heard at a distance of two or three miles. "It was the most extraordinary thing I've ever heard," Bonnici said, although he has often listened to the songs of the whales.

Even more impressive than the cries of the walrus, however, is the thrilling sound of the Weddell seals, taped in the Antarctic by Dr. Carlton Ray. It is a long, plaintive yelp, reminiscent of the howling of wolves.

Equality in the Arctic

The Arctic is the only place left on earth where the relationship between man and animal is still balanced. I mean that the large mammals have not yet been crushed and terrorized by man, despite the introduction of the rifle and the use of outboard motors. There is not yet the tragic disproportion between the hunter and the hunted which weighs so heavily upon the animals of Africa and Asia. In the Arctic, nature has interposed herself between the power of man and the fate of the animals, and she has tipped the scales in favor of the latter. The hunters' victims are hidden by snow and fog and protected by storms. Man is immobilized by the elements, threatened by the sea, paralyzed by the cold. These are things to which man's prey has adapted better and more quickly than man; and, therefore, with nature on the side of the animals and technology on that of man, the two are evenly paired.

These are the things which ran through my mind when, transfixed with cold, huddling at the bottom of Vernon's oumiak, listening to the sputtering of the motor and the whistling of the wind, we made our way through the waves toward Gambell after our encounter with the walruses. Already, our hands and feet were frozen; and we knew that, somehow, we would have to drag ourselves, and the oumiak behind us, across the belt of ice before the village. I did not see how we could manage it without one of us slipping into the freezing water. But then, we had never left the beach without my wondering the same thing, and, somehow, we usually managed the crossing without any serious accidents.

It is very easy for a man raised in the West to get into the habit of cursing the climate in the Arctic. We do not have the wisdom and patience of the Eskimos, who laugh when the wind is so strong that they must walk bent double, or when it blows away the walrus skins that they have painstakingly stretched over wood frames to dry. It takes a great deal to make an Eskimo lose his patience under the blows dealt him by nature. Perhaps it is because he is aware that nature, hard as she may sometimes be, is also generous. She has conferred on the Eskimo a living wealth equaled virtually nowhere else. The Eskimo's homeland, barren as it appears, has animal resources in abundance, and these resources are still more or less intact. Warm-blooded animals have adapted so well to life in the Arctic and Antarctic that some of them have chosen these areas as their preferred habitat and refuge. Seals, cetaceans, and walruses all find food there in greater abundance than elsewhere. For many marine mammals, the glacial waters of the earth are the pantry of the sea.

Land mammals as well as sea mammals have found a habitat in the cold regions of the North, and they have prospered there. In the winter, their coats grow long and thick as protection against the cold, and the animals build up a reserve of fat against the months when food is scarce.

One of the most remarkable of these animals is the white, or polar, bear, which, during the summer, is constantly on the move, sometimes walking and sometimes swimming, in search of food. It is a marine animal, unlike its brother bears. Its favorite food is the seal, but, on occasion, it will also eat fish. No animal of the Arctic is the polar bear's equal in strength or power, but it seldom dares attack a walrus, or even to challenge one in the water. It may be deterred by the fact that, if it attacks one walrus, it will probably be attacked in turn by the other walruses of the group.

The Eskimos affirm stubbornly that the polar bear kills sleeping walruses by clubbing them with blocks of ice. This story is so widespread, and the witnesses are listed with such precision, that it is hard to believe this is a tale invented for the entertainment of tourists. Knut Rasmussen, for one, tells us that the polar bear is capable of holding a block of ice in its enormous fore-paws and using it to crush the skull of a walrus. I cannot confirm this assertion, since neither I nor any of *Calypso*'s men have ever witnessed such an event. We can say, however, that bears are certainly able to use their fore-paws with amazing dexterity. In captivity, they have been known to throw large pieces of wood and bone. There is no reason, I suppose, why they could not throw ice with equal facility.

During the winter, some of the male bears and all of the females take shelter in caves or glacial cavities and, when their refuges are covered by the snow, their thick coats provide effective protection against the cold. They sleep throughout the winter, but only with one eye closed, so to speak. They

Following page: This patriarch refused to be dislodged from his island of ice, and he tried to intimidate us into leaving

do not hibernate in the true sense of that term, since their body temperature is not lowered perceptibly during their sojourn under the snow.

Among the other animals of the Arctic are the polar foxes, which are gray brown in summer and white in winter; and the large arctic hares, whose coats are white the entire year and whose fur is greatly prized by the Eskimos.

And, finally, the Arctic is largely populated, as I have said, by birds. In the circumpolar regions, there are more than fifty species of marine birds, some of which find their food in the sea throughout the year.

This surprising wealth of animal life in the Arctic, where man has not yet had the opportunity to massacre or to deform the animals, is the last refuge which remains untouched by human expansion and by the upheaval of planetary institutions. Whether it will survive intact into the future is another question. Man has already begun to move into the polar regions. Towns have been built to exploit resources other than those represented by the animals — oil, iron, copper. The pioneers who inhabit those settlements have already proved themselves to be the deadliest enemies of the seals, walruses, and bears.

Civilized man, with his eagerness for "development," his incomprehension of other life forms, and his machines, has already established himself at both poles. Since this is so, the odds are that the animals there will inevitably suffer the fate to which the other animals of the planet have been subjected. That is, they will be stunted in their own development, or destroyed.

Perhaps the greatest resource of the Arctic is the Eskimo himself. The Eskimo has endured everything, even the blessings of "progress," and yet remained the most contented of men. Or perhaps it would be more accurate to say that the Eskimos are infinitely more gay, more courageous, and more self-confident than the vast majority of humans. And this, despite the difficulties which the Eskimos must endure because of the arctic climate. Their unceasing good humor, which seems suspiciously akin to genuine happiness, is due, I suspect, to their preservation of a way of life the secret of which we Westerners lost centuries ago.

I am certain that there are no children loved more tenderly and cared for more assiduously than those of the Eskimos. The Eskimo children are, in effect, a guarantee for the future. For a long time, infant mortality was very high; today, therefore, children are regarded by the Eskimos as their most precious possessions. It is this new generation of Eskimo who, by effecting a reconciliation between the old traditions and the new technology, will perhaps find a way to effect the assimilation of a very old people into contemporary life.

Eleven

Burke the Walrus

The sea was still calm, and the sky without clouds. A flight of screeching boobies circled over a slab of ice floating near Vernon's oumiak. It was a perfect day to be on the water.

We were on our way, with Vernon, to witness and film the walrus hunt of the Eskimos, an event which, according to the evidence, has a history of over a thousand years' duration. While Charlemagne was lording it over Western Europe, the ancestors of Vernon and his friends were already engaging in their annual walrus hunt. Indeed, the walrus has always been too rich a resource for man to leave the animal in peace. It is estimated that, during the past two hundred years, between two and three million specimens were killed in the Bering Straits alone. Yet, while the species has diminished in numbers, it has not disappeared. Survival, in this instance, may well have depended on the walruses themselves, who chose, as their mating grounds, increasingly inaccessible areas in the polar regions.

Man has always had to kill animals in order to eat, and he always will. The fact does not free him of the contradictory emotions he feels at the sight of an animal's bloody corpse on the ground.

There was a time when an encounter between a man and an animal, especially a large animal, was at least an encounter between more or less

Once more, it was necessary for us to undertake some rather complicated maneuvers in order to reach the open water

evenly matched adversaries. But today, when man is armed with high-powered rifles, motors, walkie-talkies, and powerful binoculars, that equality no longer exists. The hunter, who had once to rely entirely on his own intelligence and skill, now has a power, conferred on him by technology, which is greater than that of any animal. Fortunately, nature has provided at least the animals of the Arctic with a last line of defense: the climate.

The annual migration of the walruses, and their passage near Gambell, is of brief duration: approximately six weeks. During that time, the foul weather usually makes it impossible for the Eskimos to hunt more than one day out of three. It is true that the modern Eskimo no longer finds it absolutely necessary to kill walruses in order to survive. He no longer depends on a supply of frozen walrus meat, buried in the ice, as his sole source of food during the winter. Walrus is still eaten, of course, but it is supplemented by food which arrives regularly from the mainland by air.

If the walrus has lost something of its value as food, it has retained its usefulness as a source of other materials. The walrus hunt of the Eskimos today is justified by the necessity of procuring hides with which to cover their oumiaks. "This year," Vernon told me, "I am going to need at least six new skins." He was referring, of course, to the skins of female walruses.

The hides of young walruses are also necessary as a source of ropes and lines. The hide is cut into long spirals, which are then worked and braided into lines of great strength.

Therefore, from the beginning of the hunting season, the inhabitants of Gambell hunt the female walruses and the young walruses and spare the large males.

Walruses must be approached with caution. It happens occasionally that these animals will attack an oumiak and rip it open with their tusks

Head-hunters of the Arctic

The most murderous aspect of the walrus hunt is not the quest of the Eskimos for hides but for ivory. Since walrus is no longer the animal sent by Providence to keep the Eskimos from starving, it has become a source of profit, the raw material of a thriving industry.

As we drew near, the walruses slid into the water

There are practically no controls in the hunt for walrus tusks. Many of the animals are killed only for their ivory, and it is not unusual to find the body of a dead walrus intact except for its head. The hunters of meat have become the head-hunters of the Arctic. It is especially deplorable that female animals, in addition to being killed for food, are also killed merely for the tusks.

Ivory carving has become an industry among the Eskimos, but there are no quality standards, and these carvings are undertaken purely for profit. The most infantile scratching on a tusk is considered "carving," since even the clumsiest image enables a tusk to qualify as "carved ivory" and to be exported.

It happens occasionally that the annual walrus hunt cannot be undertaken because of the weather. One year, when the walruses were passing before Gambell, there was a violent storm which continued without interruption, and the oumiaks were unable to leave the shore. In that year, the total kill of the village consisted of one walrus. It was a disastrous year for Gambell.

On this occasion, nature had been more generous to the Eskimos. Several walruses had already been killed, and there would be many more. Now, following the oumiak of the hunting party, we witnessed a scene that would be repeated perhaps four hundred times during the season. It was not an attractive scene; but, compared to the kind of useless and vainglorious hunting in which Americans and Europeans indulge for reasons best known to themselves, it had at least the saving grace of being necessary to the well-being of the Eskimos.

The hunters' victim was a female. The females are easily recognizable because they are accompanied by their young. The calf usually swims alongside the mother, or is carried on the mother's back. The ultimate tragedy perhaps is that the shooting of a walrus mother does not always result in gain to the Eskimos. Many of the victims either dive, or sink to the bottom and are lost. Every year, some 11,700 walruses are killed along the American and Soviet coasts, and it is estimated that at least half that number disappear after they have been shot.

This is a loss which the world can ill afford. Walruses are not prolific animals. A female is not fertile until she reaches the age of six or seven years, and then she carries her young for thirteen months. At the present rate of reproduction, one walrus is born for every two adults killed. And, naturally, since a baby walrus cannot possibly survive without its mother, the offspring of the hunters' victims inevitably die. It may be that the fortunate ones are those which are captured; for them, at least, the agony is brief.

Killer Whales and Bears

The walrus has few enemies other than man. They are so large, so powerful, and so agile in the sea that not many animals dare attack them there. The only exception seems to be the killer whale, the most formidable predator in the sea, which attacks not only walruses but whales as well. The killer whale attacks in groups and attempts to bite the walrus on the upper lip and drag it toward the bottom. But the killer whale is not always the victor. A walrus is quite capable of dealing a mortal blow even to such a fearsome attacker. It uses its tusks to great advantage, with a technique which has often been observed. Our Eskimo friends told us that they had seen a walrus seize a seal between its forward fins and then repeatedly strike the seal with its tusks until it was dead.

The polar bear feeds chiefly on seals, but it sometimes also attacks walruses when the latter are on the ice, where they move slowly and awkwardly. In the water, however, the bear gives the walrus a wide berth. It will not even go into the water when a group of walruses is in the area.

The hunt which we were following took place according to the traditions of the Eskimos. Once the female walrus had been shot, the hunters began shouting and gesticulating until they had brought themselves to a pitch of excitement. This enthusiasm was intended to commemorate the hunts of earlier times, when the Eskimos killed walruses by approaching them in kayaks and then spearing them with harpoons to which air bladders had been attached. Such an undertaking was quite dangerous and warranted a certain degree of pride. The walrus had to be struck behind its head, and if the harpoon missed its mark, the walrus often turned on the kayak and ripped it to shreds. In such cases, the hunters did not always escape.

The modern Eskimo uses firearms, and the killing of a walrus is not nearly so dangerous as it once was. Still, old traditions die hard, and our hunters stood, laughing and congratulating one another, on the slab of ice where the dead female lay. Then one of the men drew his long glistening knife. As leader, it was his privilege to open the animal's stomach with a single, long, straight cut, and then to make a crosscut. The blood poured out, and the other hunters began skinning the walrus.

The Orphan

Meanwhile, the dead mother's calf had taken to the water and was swimming about aimlessly. We fished it out and hoisted it into Vernon's

We take aboard a baby walrus whose mother was killed by a hunter

Right: Two divers undertake to teach Burke how to swim

Our foundling dragged himself across the snow while making a strange, barking sound. We named him Burke — after that sound

oumiak. The fact is, there was nothing else we could do. The baby walrus would surely have died if left on its own. So, we saved its life. (Ironically, it eventually turned out that the young walrus would return the favor.)

The young animal did not struggle, and it showed not the slightest sign of fear. In fact, it had swum toward the oumiak, probably mistaking the floating object for its mother. Vernon had helped matters along by barking like a mother walrus.

As soon as the walrus was in the boat it snuggled up to one of the divers. The black vinyl diving suit is not unlike the skin of a female walrus, and the animal was searching for a substitute mother. It needed the warmth of another mammal; in this case, human warmth. It not only accepted man but became instantly and wildly attached to him. The calf's need to be loved and petted was so desperate that no one could resist it.

Meanwhile, on the ice, the carving of the walrus was proceeding at a pace which astonished us. The animal's body, subjected to five or six razor-sharp knives simultaneously, was literally coming apart before our eyes, but in a manner so orderly and methodical that there was no confusion and no waste. Even the blood was carefully drained into a pail.

We heard the walrus's bones breaking, and its tendons were removed to serve as the material for lines and thread. Finally, large, thick slabs of black meat were cut. They would be cut into thin slices later and dried in the sun.

The heart was removed. It was enormous. According to Vernon's estimate, it weighed between twenty and twenty-five pounds.

The intestines would also be used. Emptied of their content of yellowish excrement, then filled with blood, they would become walrus blood sausage. For the moment, they lay in a limp heap on the ice, dripping a greenish liquid and emanating a disagreeable odor. The ice, which had been immaculate before, was now covered with waste, fat, and oil; and the men slipped as they worked.

As efficiently as the Eskimos worked, their concern was not entirely pragmatic. Before beginning the carving of the walrus, they had harkened back to the time when the survival of their people had depended entirely upon the walrus hunt, and they had made a ritual offering to the gods. A piece of that black flesh and that thick white fat had been cut off of the animal and thrown into the sea. The Eskimos had performed this act with an apologetic smile, torn between their determination to be thoroughly modern men and the superstitions which still lurked deep within them.

An Attack

The butchering of the walrus, however justified, was beginning to turn our stomachs. The stench was overwhelming. We decided to inspect the neighborhood so as to observe the animals. Bonnici started up the outboard and, at slow speed, began moving through the floes. The baby walrus was snuggled happily in Prezelin's arms, apparently unaffected by its status as an orphan. From time to time, it made a clucking sound, which we interpreted as signifying hunger. But contact with the human body seemed to reassure it, and Prezelin's petting calmed the animal.

We headed toward a large group of walruses lying on the ice. The animals were packed together so densely that they seemed to be in two layers. As we drew near, we decided on the tactics to be adopted. We would first move past the ice in the boat, as close as possible to the walruses, while using our cameras. Then we would return for some close-ups on the ice. Finally, we would try to get some underwater footage.

We had learned from experience that these floating islands of ice are often surrounded by submerged platforms on which oumiaks sometimes run aground. Therefore, one of the divers stationed himself in the bow. It was his job to make certain that the water was deep enough for the boat's draught.

We began, as we had planned, by moving past the island at a distance of about three feet. We stared at the walruses, and they stared back at us. The cameras whirled. Like a widening ripple on a pond, alarm spread over the herd. Heads rose, tusks were brandished, bodies reared up. Then, very suddenly, about half of the herd — that nearer to us — plunged into the water. The ice island, relieved of the weight over half of its surface, bobbed madly in the water, raising the submerged platform on our side. We heard the outboard's propeller strike bottom. Then, an instant later, the oumiak itself was raised out of the water and we were sitting — perhaps not on dry land but at least on wet ice.

About fifty walruses were lying in a semicircle, quite close to the oumiak. Some of them remained asleep and emitted a few groans. Others rose and began moving toward us, clumsily but at a surprisingly fast pace. I could not take my eyes from those long, sharp tusks coming toward us like parallel rows of daggers glittering in the sunlight. Behind the tusks, the walruses' huge, muscular necks moved rhythmically. Then they began their charge, heavily, irresistibly, like a line of tanks moving across an open field.

They were a few seconds away from the oumiak when the walrus orphan began shrieking at the top of his lungs. He was still too small to roar. His cry was high-pitched: the cry of a child in distress. Immediately, the attacking walruses halted in their tracks. Sounds, soft sounds now, rose from their ranks. They waddled about indecisively for a few seconds, their heads moving, their tusks lowered. Then, they lay down on the ice.

We do not know exactly what had happened. I can only record the facts: the cries of the baby walrus and the sudden abandonment of the attack by the adult walruses were simultaneous. The Eskimos assured us afterward that walruses never attack an oumiak which is carrying a baby walrus.

A few seconds after this incident, a thick, white fog, like a wall of cotton, settled over the island. We could no longer see the walruses, and they could no longer see us. Dorado and Bonnici leaped from the oumiak, dragged the boat back to the water, and hurriedly climbed aboard. The outboard carried us out into the sea, or rather, into the opaque layer which covered the surface. It was as though we were in an airplane moving through the clouds. Visibility was near zero. We were constantly obliged to circle about in order to avoid the blocks of floating ice which suddenly loomed up before us.

Frankly, we were rather worried. We had not yet found the ice island where our Eskimo friends were slaughtering their walrus, and, without Vernon, who was on the island, it was likely that we would be unable to find our way back to Gambell. St. Lawrence seemed very far away. Surely, I told myself, Vernon and the others would realize what had happened when we did not return for them. Eskimos are dependable, responsible people. They never

abandon a friend in need. At the same time, I could not help blaming ourselves for our situation. We had been careless and imprudent. If we were lost,
it was out own doing.

Then, unexpectedly, there was a rift in the fog, and we saw the island
behind us. There were men on it, moving about and waving. We had passed
them in the fog, without seeing or hearing them. Quickly, before the rift
closed, we made a half-circle and reached the floe. The Eskimos were smiling
good-naturedly.

After the walrus meat had been loaded aboard the oumiak, we set out
again into the fog. But now, everything seemed simple and safe. We had
found our friends, and there was no longer any danger.

The way back to Gambell, however, was filled with obstacles. The
ghostly white icebergs, perceived dimly through the fog, were quite real. They
were beautiful but undeniably dangerous.

The baby walrus was unmindful of any danger. He slept most of the
way, and when he awoke it was only to push his head against us, which was
his way of asking to be petted.

The oumiaks were in constant communication by walkie-talkie, but the
messages were limited to a single sound: "Ah, ah, ah." We concluded that ah-
ah-ah meant, "I am OK. Are you OK? Let's go on."

Despite these repeated assurances, passed from boat to boat, navigation
did not always go smoothly. Vernon, although he claimed that he navigated
by his nose, had a handsome compass which he consulted frequently and
furtively. Gambell lay to the south of our position. Vernon therefore headed
southeast, to make certain that we would reach the broad side of the island
and not skirt it in the fog. When we reached the ice along the coast of St.
Lawrence, he did not tack about until we were a few yards from shore. Eskimos are very adept at distinguishing in the darkness the slabs of ice which
float out from the shore and which have not yet broken into pieces. The importance of such distinctions is evidenced by the fact that the Eskimo language contains some two hundred and fifty words designating the different
kinds of ice.

We reached Gambell at 4 A.M. Our first duty ashore was to take care of
the baby walrus.* We dug a hole in the ice for him, about four feet deep, and
surrounded it with a protective fence. Then we fell asleep.

---

*Ed Asper, an expert on walruses who was attached to Marineland of the Pacific, was extremely helpful in
advising us on the care of the baby walrus. I should also note that we obtained a permit for keeping the
animal in captivity.

Right: Burke is still a beginner in the water and he is reluctant to leave his friend, Louis
Prezelin

Bath and Bottle

The divers named our baby walrus Burke, a name taken from the guttural sound of the animal's bark.

Burke was very attached to all of us. He obviously had found friends to take the place of his mother. He was very curious, and he made constant use of his whiskers, which were very sensitive tactile organs, to explore the world around him.

I do not think that there has ever been a baby walrus who received more loving care than Burke. In the wild, a calf is bathed by its mother. Now, that task devolved upon us. It was not difficult. Once Burke had been washed, we rubbed him with snow, which both dried him off and finished cleaning him.

After bathing the walrus, we gave him his bottle. Until recently, it was difficult to keep baby sea mammals alive, but today we are able to mix a formula which is very similar to the milk of the mother walrus. The recipe calls for a mixture of shells, cream, corn oil, salt, calcium, and vitamins. Burke was able to drink two quarts of this mixture at a time. Afterward, he slept, snoring. Ed Asper was convinced that Burke even dreamed.

Love and Affection

Burke was never happy when alone. He had become unbelievably attached to us, and as soon as we left him alone, he whimpered and barked like a dog left alone at home.

He followed us around Gambell, moving clumsily over the ice. Sometimes he was so eager to catch up to us that he fell into holes and was not able to climb out unaided. Then, like a child, he cried until we came to pull him out. It had required millions of years for the limbs of these mammals, who once lived on land, to evolve into fins. The transformation has been so effective that walruses, both young and old, move on land only with difficulty. Burke's "webbed feet" obliged him to waddle and pivot on his hind legs, which gave him a very comical appearance.

He required affection even more desperately than food, and his efforts to keep up with us were so touching that one of the divers usually ended up carrying him.

Burke had his favorites among us. Ed Asper, who spent the most time caring for Burke, was not as successful as Giacoletto and Bonnici in this respect; especially not when Giacoletto and Bonnici's hands were permeated with the smell of the mollusks and vitamins that they fed him twice a day.

Burke was particularly happy when he was able to lie down at full length against one of the men in a diving suit and rub his whiskers against the diver's face. "I've never seen an animal as lovable and affectionate as that walrus," François Dorado said. "He used to kiss us with his whiskers and use his flippers to hold on to us."

A Swimming Lesson

While Burke was becoming accustomed to his semicaptivity and learning to live with us, the weather took a decided turn for the worse. For a time, we could neither go out in the oumiak nor dive in the water off Gambell. When the sun finally broke through, we decided that it was time for Burke to go into the sea, which meant that the divers would also have to venture out into the icy water. Burke was protected against the cold by a layer of fat, but, even with this accessory, baby walruses have no natural attraction for the water. They are taught to swim by their mothers, by holding on to her and climbing onto her back. Our orphan had completely forgotten his natural habitat. He was afraid of the water, and he had already forgotten how to swim. Dorado had to take him in his arms and put him in the water. Burke panicked, like a man drowning, and clutched at everyone within reach, the cameramen as well as Dorado.

Christian Bonnici finally became Burke's swimming and diving instructor. He began by teaching the animal to swim slowly at the surface, among the other divers. Burke was a true beginner. He did everything backward. He held his breath when he was on the surface, and he swallowed water when he was diving. He did not enjoy the experience, and he felt safe again only when he was on Bonnici's back, holding on to his arm as though he were clutching his mother's flippers.

When Burke had regained his calm, Bonnici pressed his neck gently to force him into the water, and then immediately put him on his back again. He repeated this tactic until, gradually, Burke lost his fear of the water and was able to dive to the bottom. The walrus was now more or less at home in the water, thanks to the determination of the divers to be adequate substitute mothers.

When Burke swam rather far from the divers, he barked until someone went out to get him. He loved especially to swim with Prezelin, and he used to hold on to Louis's mask and rub his whiskers against the diver's face.

Once he felt sure of himself, Burke went into the water whenever we wished him to do so, and he became an excellent film actor. We soon noticed

Burke became very fond of our divers, and they were all equally attached to him. Here, he takes his bottle under the supervision of Philippe Cousteau and is petted by Jacques Renoir

that he liked to dig on the bottom for food. But, as yet, he did not know his limitations in the water, and he wanted to remain on the bottom longer than he was able. Then the divers practically had to drag him back to the surface with them.

Baby walruses, like the offspring of most mammals, require an extensive course of instruction before they are able to fend for themselves in the world. When they are born, they already have long points at the tips of their fingers, and very full whiskers like a brush on their upper lips. They nurse until the age of two or two and a half years. Also at the age of two, their tusks begin to develop.

It is difficult for someone who has not seen it to conceive of the degree of affection that a mother walrus feels for her offspring. The walrus may be the most striking example of maternal love in the world of mammals. She never allows her calf to wander out of her sight; and it happens frequently that a mother will throw herself between a spearman and her calf and take the blow in its stead.

If the baby walrus is wounded or even killed, the mother does not abandon it but carries it around with her, moaning all the while. If a mother senses danger, she tries to push her young before her, toward the bottom; and if the calf struggles, she carries it safely between her forward fins. In moments of tranquility, the mother walrus and her calf often rub noses and fins.

Obviously, the amount of care and training that Burke would require before he was an adult was beyond our means. Finally, and sadly, we turned him over to Ed Asper, who took him back to the Marineland of the Pacific, where he was to remain for at least two years while Ed continued his education.

The thaw now accelerated in the spring warmth, and the difference here, in a land imprisoned by ice, was more striking than elsewhere. It is more like the liberation of nature than a simple thaw. One morning, we saw the true sign of that liberation: between the beach and the ice surrounding St. Lawrence Island, there was a stream of dark water marking the shoreline like the pen of a geographer's drawing. A small island of rock had freed itself of ice and seemed to be floating in the sea. The line of icebergs which obstructed part of the horizon was shattered. It was as though the earth was struggling to be reborn.

The chaotic blocks of ice, which had enclosed Gambell like a wall, now separated and drifted away on the water. Vernon shrugged. "The wind will bring them back," he predicted.

It did not matter whether they returned or not. So far as I was concerned, the winter was over. I watched the blocks move northward in the current, thinking that we were finally rid of them.

The ice gradually melted on land and slid into the water. The beach, which had been a stretch of ice, now became a surface of black pebbles. The departing ice also revealed other things along the shore: nameless wrecks of boats, scrap metal, and battered metal drums.

Along Gambell's only street and around every house, we began to see miserable, twisted garbage of indestructible, unburnable plastic, and heaps of metal. All that the Eskimos had thrown away, through whim, negligence, or lack of foresight, had been covered by the snow, and the village had appeared immaculate. Now, the merciless sun exposed the trash heaps of Gambell once more.

The time for hunting walruses had passed, and still the elders of the village maintained their watch on the beach. The hunt was over, but everything concerning walruses was still the focal point of their lives and the food of their minds. This year, the hunt had been successful. There had been a distribution of an average of one walrus to every Eskimo house.

The passage of the walruses en route to the north was practically over. Only one block of ice, drifting in the sea, was still dotted with the animals. Soon, the ice boxcars of the walruses would also melt in the sun unless they first reached the southern glacial boundary. Meanwhile, the growling males, the worried females, and the curious calves were on their way to the Chukchi Sea, where they would find an abundance of the mollusks which they loved.

In the village of Gambell, there was a feast to mark the end of the hunt. On that occasion, the main attraction was Louis Prezelin, who created a sensation by allowing himself to be tossed in a walrus hide by four sturdy Eskimos. This is a form of entertainment traditional among the Eskimos, and they were delighted to see a Frenchman participate willingly in their games. Louis assures us that tossing warms up the man who is tossed and keeps him in shape.

Such traditions are still alive at Gambell, but one wonders how much longer they will survive. Can we simultaneously offer a higher standard of living to the Eskimos, educate them in the ways of the West, and still preserve their culture? Is conflict inevitable between "civilization" and respect for the past of a people?

These are some of the questions that I put to Mr. Walter Hickel, member of the Alaskan Council and former Secretary of the Interior. "The most important thing," Mr. Hickel told me, "is to leave the Eskimos free to live as they wish to live. They must live in harmony with the sea. We have the responsibility for watching over them; yet, we have to be careful not to protect them so much that they no longer enjoy the kind of life that they have taken thousands of years to make for themselves; a life which is in conformity with this climate and with the animals of the Arctic."

Twelve

Epilogue

This book, like others in the series, is the story of our attempts to make friends of the animals in the sea, and to turn these friends into diving companions. In this instance, all of the animals were marine mammals, that is, warm-blooded animals, equipped with lungs, who are more similar to man in many respects than are fishes.

Our approach in this endeavor was not to force friendship upon the animals but rather to come to deserve their trust. We tried to avoid all forms of constraint, all forms of "training" which might turn the animal into something which it was not. By loving the animals, we attempted to awaken a response in them which would cause them to love us.

We dare not say that we were entirely successful.

The most moving of our experiences was undoubtedly that of Pepito and Christobald; but even with these sea lions, who came eventually to trust us, we did not attain complete success. Christobald died because he wished to regain his freedom. After his escape, he attempted to return to human society,

Following page: The walrus is a creature as enigmatic as it is enormous, but we ended by developing a certain sympathy for it

but the humans he found did not know how to care for him. Such care requires much experience and much devotion, and I am afraid that our lives on dry land have made us insensitive to the needs of creatures of the sea.

As for Pepito, he left us in order to return to his own kind. The decision to let him go was a difficult one, but it is one which I have never regretted.

The elephant seals, unlike the sea lions, responded not at all to our offer of friendship. It is true that they did not flee, and they were aggressive only when provoked. But their immense weight, their slowness of comprehension, and their wariness in the water all worked against the kind of relationship that *Calypso*'s men had in mind. In other words, they were not ideal companions. Yet even the elephant seals taught us a great deal merely by ignoring our presence and continuing, undisturbed, their lives of love and combat on the beaches of Guadalupe. They reminded us that there is indeed a chasm which separates man and animal, and that if that chasm is to be bridged, it must be man who does it by means of understanding. But before we can understand, we must know; and to know, we must love. We must love life in all its forms, even in those which we find least attractive. I am happy, even proud, to say that, despite their appearance, their roars and their smell, the elephant seals ended by winning our sympathy.

Walruses, like elephant seals, are enigmatic creatures. But, with them, at least it was easier to find some common ground for understanding, in the maternal affection of walrus mothers and the need for affection of baby walruses. In this respect, Burke was, to us, the symbol of gentleness and of an emotional life in the harsh, icy world of the Arctic.

The attempt to establish a common life between man on the one hand and pinnipeds or cetaceans on the other is not an experiment which can be expected to produce quick results. The attempt, in fact, has only just begun. It required uncounted thousands of years for man to learn to approach land animals, and still not everyone is convinced that it is better to protect these animals than to kill them.

In the sea, the task that awaits us is even more complex. The animals that we must learn to approach and to live with are the inhabitants of a milieu, a world, that is alien to us and that we have hardly begun to explore. The initiation of man into marine life is far from being finished. Our senses and our minds are still firmly bound to dry land. Yet the day will come when we will embark on a new phase of the human adventure; and then we will be in need of friends in the sea with whom we may begin to communicate.

There are many marine mammals, other than sea lions and elephant seals and walruses, which have demonstrated an affinity for man. The so-called blackfish, or pilot whale, for example, which we have encountered on several occasions while diving, is capable of extraordinary feats. The American Navy makes use of them to find practice torpedoes in the sea. And the killer whale, or orc, as we have pointed out in our book on whales, is a model of affection and loyalty to man, and it is perhaps the most gifted of our marine friends.

Attitudes toward the animals around us have begun to change, and it seems likely that that evolution will continue, however slowly. Affection and respect for animals occupy ever-larger places in our lives. Historically, the importance of animals to man has been based not on life but on death. The animal was man's prey, whether it fell in the primeval forest under the hand of a man with a stone ax, or in a Chicago slaughterhouse. The animals who shared our lives, rather than having conferred on us the benefit of their deaths, were few indeed beyond the dog and the cat. Yet, there is no animal incapable of becoming man's friend. This holds as true of the killer whale, despite its reputed "ferocity," as it does of the mighty lion.

One can only hope that the truth of this statement will be recognized before we succeed in depriving ourselves, forever, of the animals who are our fellow tenants on the planet earth. There was a time when hunting, that sanguinary expression of love, was the chief enemy of animal life. Now, it seems likely that pollution and the human-population explosion are sometimes more harmful than hunters. And this is why the establishment of a new relationship between man and the marine mammals does not depend upon a few more or less successful experiments. Such a relationship is part of a complex of conditions affecting the progress we make in our exploration of the seas and the attitude of respect which we bring with us into those seas.

It means nothing to strike up a friendship with a sea lion or a dolphin if, at the same time, we are destroying their last refuges along our coasts and our islands. It is an exercise in vanity and absurdity to try to communicate with a killer whale and then to put it on exhibition in an aquatic zoo as a circus freak.

The world of living beings is a *whole*. As a whole, it is indispensable to the ecological balance of the planet and to the psychological equilibrium of man. Any real solution to the problem of the environment must therefore be a global solution, effective simultaneously at the scientific, technological, legislative, political, and international levels. If we pretend otherwise, we are not being honest with ourselves or with those who will come after us.

"We must learn to love life, even in its least attractive manifestations."

ACKNOWLEDGMENTS

We would like to express our gratitude to all those who have helped in the preparation of this book, and especially to the following: Ed Asper and John Prescott, Marineland of the Pacific; John J. Burns, a biologist with the Department of Fish and Game of the State of Alaska; Francis Fay of the Arctic Research Medical Center; Carleton Ray of John Hopkins University; and to the United States Marine Research Laboratory at Point Barrow.

PHOTO CREDITS

In the preparation of this volume, as in the others of the series, Carmela Lambert's skill in working with photographic material has been of inestimable value. We owe her a special debt of gratitude.

The photographs in the book were taken by Ron Church, François Dorado, André Laban, Claude Millet, Guy Jouas, Louis Prézelin, and Jacques Renoir.

Several of the surface photographs were selected from the private collections of various members of *Calypso*'s team.

Iconography: Marie-Noëlle Favier.

The sketches which appear in the Glossary and the Appendices were executed by Jean-Charles Roux.

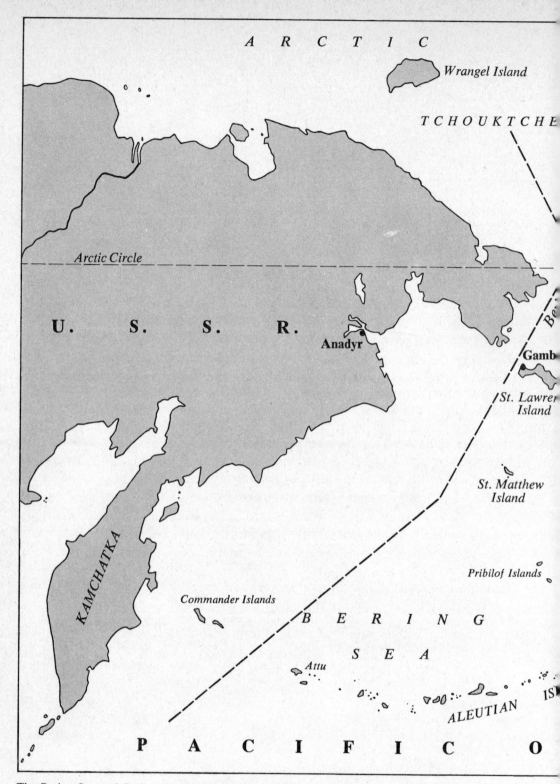

The Bering Sea and Bering Straits, showing Round Island, Walrus Island (both in Bristol Bay) and, at the entry to the strait, St. Lawrence Island and the village of Gambell. The dotted line shows the boundary between the United States and the U.S.S.R.

O C E A N

Barrow

B E A U F O R T   S E A

E A

ut

U N I T E D   S T A T E S

C
A
N
A
D
A

A L A S K A

Nome

Yukon

Norton Sound

Mt. McKinley
▲ 6193

Anchorage

nivak
and

Togiak

Round Island

Juneau

Bristol Bay

Kodiak
Island

G U L F

O F

A L A S K A

Alexander Archipelago

OS

C E A N

0   500 km

APPENDICES

Appendix One

Calypso and the AQUA-LUNG®

For all practical purposes, the use of the Aqua-Lung and the cruises of *Calypso* are inseparable. The invention of the Aqua-Lung made it possible for man to undertake the exploration of the depths; and *Calypso*, essentially an oceanographic research vessel, by use of the Aqua-Lung, has made important contributions to man's knowledge of those depths. *Calypso*'s contributions have been increased also by use of the two diving saucers, or minisubs, which are kept aboard permanently.

The Aqua-Lung

The introduction of the Aqua-Lung represented a decisive step forward in man's life in the sea. It replaced the old diving suit, with its heavy helmet and its airlines running to the surface, which could be used only by trained personnel, which was difficult to handle, and which placed narrow limits on the diver's field of activity.

The Aqua-Lung, or SCUBA (Self-Contained Underwater Breathing Apparatus) was invented in 1943 by Jacques-Yves Cousteau and an engineer,

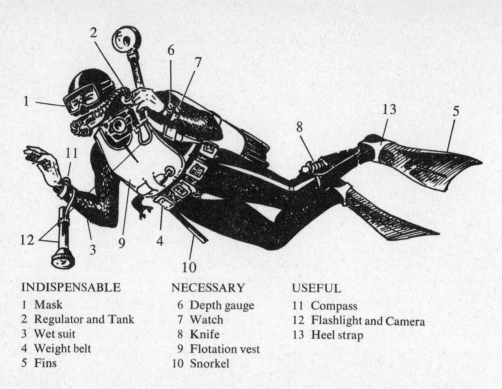

INDISPENSABLE	NECESSARY	USEFUL
1 Mask	6 Depth gauge	11 Compass
2 Regulator and Tank	7 Watch	12 Flashlight and Camera
3 Wet suit	8 Knife	13 Heel strap
4 Weight belt	9 Flotation vest	
5 Fins	10 Snorkel	

Cousteau-Gagnan self-contained underwater breathing apparatus, Mistral type, and diving accessories.

Émile Gagnan. It is an "open-circuit" apparatus, that is, the used air is expelled directly into the water. The air is provided, not in continuous fashion, but only when the diver inhales.

The equipment includes one or more air tanks which are strapped onto the diver's back, and the flow of air is controlled by a regulator which delivers air when the diver inhales and which assures that the pressure of the air delivered corresponds to that of the water surrounding the diver. When the diver exhales, the used air is fed into the water through an exhaust located under the hood of the regulator. Two flexible tubes run from the mouthpiece to the regulator. One of these is for inhalation, the other, for exhalation.

The accessories used with the Aqua-Lung are the mask, the webbed fins originally designed by Commandant de Corlieu, and a belt weighted with several pounds of lead which serve to neutralize the buoyancy of the human body.

This simple, entirely automatic, and easy-to-use apparatus has opened up the sea to man, at least to a certain depth, and has made it possible for him to undertake a true exploration of the seas. The work done in that area in the past two decades was feasible only because of the Aqua-Lung.

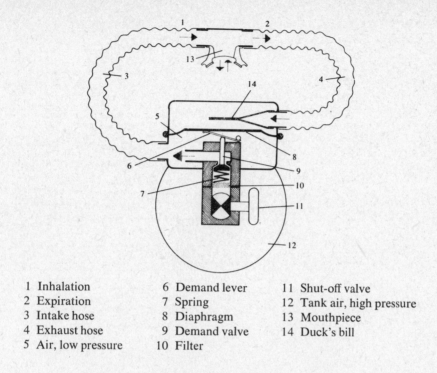

1 Inhalation
2 Expiration
3 Intake hose
4 Exhaust hose
5 Air, low pressure

6 Demand lever
7 Spring
8 Diaphragm
9 Demand valve
10 Filter

11 Shut-off valve
12 Tank air, high pressure
13 Mouthpiece
14 Duck's bill

Diagram of the Cousteau-Gagnan regulator

A new model of the Aqua-Lung has been designed especially for *Calypso*'s divers. It includes a hydrodynamic casing around the air tanks and a helmet into which a headlight and an underwater ultrasonic telephone are incorporated. A shark stick is attached to the casing, within easy reach.

Man, even though he has learned to operate independently in the sea, is

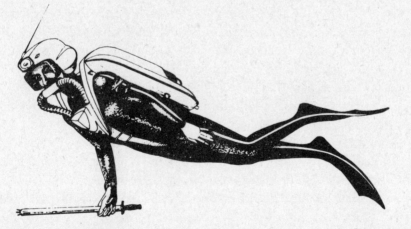

Our new self-contained hydrodynamic diving suit, with helmet and built-in telephone. The diver is holding a shark stick

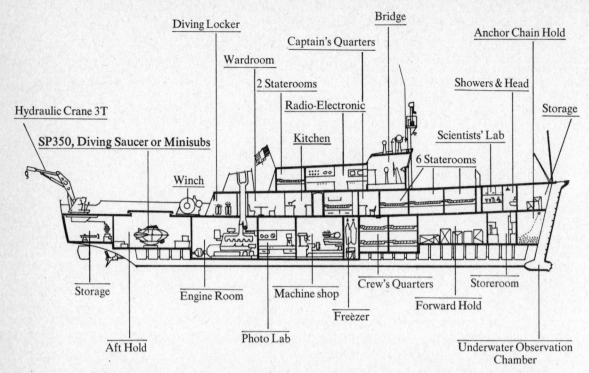

Calypso, a former mine sweeper constructed in the United States, has been modified several times for purposes of oceanographic research. The bridge and chartroom have been entirely transformed, and cabins have been added forward. The aft hole serves as a garage for our minisubs.

still susceptible to two of the dangers with which the users of the old-style diving suits always had to contend: rapture of the depths and decompression accidents.

Rapture of the depths is a form of narcosis, induced by the presence of nitrogen, which seriously impedes a diver's reasoning processes. It afflicts some divers at a depth of about 125 feet and others at greater depths and after a longer period of time. Some first become aware of the onset of this narcosis only when it is too late. The diver's threshold of susceptibility, however, can be pushed by several hundred feet by replacing the nitrogen in his breathing mixture by a lighter gas, such as helium.

Decompression accidents, on the other hand, are due to the fact that, during a dive, gas from the diver's air tends to go into solution in the diver's blood. If the diver rises to the surface too quickly, this gas comes out of solution in the form of bubbles in his bloodstream. The result is decompression sickness, which is more or less serious depending on the speed of the ascent, the depth from which the diver began the ascent, and the amount of time spent at that depth.

Decompression sickness may be prevented by timing the ascent in such a way that gas is diffused normally. For that purpose, tables have been worked out which indicate the number and duration of the pauses, or stages, that a diver must make during his ascent, according to the depth he reached and the time he spent at that depth.

If a dive has been very brief, these stages are not necessary, since the diver's system did not have time to absorb a dangerous quantity of gas. But, as depth and duration increase, so does the time required for decompression.

The phenomenon of decompression was our reason for experimenting with our "undersea houses." In the course of that experiment, a diver's body became saturated with gas after a few hours, and it was allowed to remain so, regardless of the amount of time he spent at the depth of the houses. The diver decompressed only after several days, that is, when he regained the surface at the end of the experiment which ran for several days — or, as in the case of Conshelf III, after a month spent on the bottom. Thus, it was possible for a team of divers to remain in the water for an extended period of time, at the price of only one ascent and one decompression. "Pay as you leave," Paul Bert called it.

The use of a decompression chamber makes it possible for a diver, during his ascent, to remain at the same pressure as that of the depth at which he was working. Then, back on the surface, he can be decompressed gradually and under medical supervision. In this case, the diver may be given oxygen when he attains a pressure equivalent to that which exists at a depth of less than forty feet.

Calypso

In 1947 and 1948, when we were discussing what sort of vessel would be best for exploring the seas and testing the techniques we had devised, we could not have imagined anything more suitable than *Calypso*. She is a former mine sweeper, built in the United States for the British in 1942. After the war, I was able to buy her in Malta, as war surplus, thanks mainly to the generosity of a British patron of learning, Loel Guinness.

As ships go, *Calypso* is small: 143 feet in length, with a beam of 24 feet. She is a vessel of 329 tons, very solidly built, with a double hull of wood, double planking, and very narrowly spaced timbers. She is superbly easy to handle, and her shallow draft enables her to maneuver in and out of treacherous coral reefs with a minimum of trouble. Her two engines and propellers give her a speed of ten and a half knots.

It was necessary to make extensive alterations before the mine sweeper could become an oceanographic laboratory. We added a false stem at the bow: a well which goes down about eight feet below the water line. It has eight portholes which we use to see and to film what is going on in the water, even when *Calypso* is moving. In addition, a double mast of light metal was built as far forward as possible on deck. This serves as a tower for our radar antenna and as a sort of very useful upper bridge from which to observe and direct a difficult passage.

Calypso normally carries a team of about thirty persons — in very cramped quarters because of the enormous amount of equipment required by our work.

Calypso's equipment is unequaled by that of any other oceanographic vessel: about twenty scuba outfits; a brace of underwater "scooters"; a "wet submarine"; two minisubs (our diving saucers), and numerous small boats such as our unsinkable metal runabouts, our inflatable rafts (the zodiacs), and our lifeboats, which inflate automatically when placed into the water, as well as a large amount of filmmaking equipment such as cameras, projectors, floodlights, cables, and so forth. In addition, several laboratories and aquariums have been installed. One of the latter is designed to keep the water in the aquarium from rolling, no matter how heavy the seas — a point of some importance; for fishes, like humans, are subject to seasickness.

We have a closed-circuit-television system, by means of which we can see everything that happens either on the ship or in the water. We have an ultrasonic telephone for communicating with the diving saucers and the divers and for the divers to be able to communicate with one another. We have tape recorders and underwater microphones for recording the sounds of marine animals. And, of course, we have all the latest navigational aids, including a special sonar for use in very deep water.

Calypso's expeditions are not financed by any public or private subsidy. The Oceanographic Museum of Monaco, to which we refer frequently in this series of books, lends *Calypso* its support, but it is scientific, not financial, support. *Calypso* is sponsored by a foundation set up by Captain Cousteau in 1950, *Les Campagnes Océanographiques Fraçaises.* The sole funds available to this foundation derive from book and television royalties, royalties from industry, and fees for research undertaken on behalf of various commercial enterprises.

Calypso's first expedition, her maiden voyage, was made in 1951, to the Red Sea. Her next mission was in the Mediterranean, off Marseilles, at Grand Congloué, where she took part in an archaeological dig, the subject of which was a Roman ship of the third century B.C. Since then, she has traveled

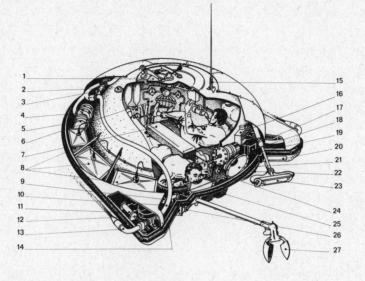

The SP-350 Diving Saucer (or Minisub)

1. Entry hatch
2. Wide-range portholes
3. Water distributor (right or left, for water jets)
4. Pump
5. Electric engine (2 hp.)
6. Interior
7. Water ballast
8. Submersible batteries
9. Control lever for pincer arm
10. Jet tube
11. Lever for front and rear jets
12. Transducer
13. Jets
14. Headlights
15. Radio antenna
16. Contact box
17. Upper transducer
18. Forward transducer
19. Forward mercury-equilibrium apparatus
20. Flash apparatus
21. Portholes
22. Sample basket
23. Telescopic projector
24. Film and photo porthole
25. Detachable kentledge
26. Photostereo apparatus
27. Pincer arm

through the Indian Ocean, and through the Atlantic and the Caribbean, shooting films — notably *The Silent World of Jacques Cousteau* — and undertaking scientific missions. Among the latter was an exciting photographic expedition, undertaken in collaboration with Professor Harold Edgerton of the Massachusetts Institute of Technology, to study various depressions in the ocean floor.

Calypso's last major expedition lasted from 1967 to 1971 and took her 140,000 nautical miles across the Mediterranean, the Red Sea, the Indian

Ocean, the Atlantic, and the Pacific, then northward to the Bering Straits. In the course of that expedition, we shot some twenty-four films for world television.

After a brief layover at Marseilles (during which we shot several more films in the Mediterranean), *Calypso,* on September 29, 1972, set out on a new adventure: a six-month expedition to the Antarctic, to study the effects of commercial hunting and toxic chemicals on the warm-blooded animals most vulnerable to such abuses: blue whales, humpback whales, right whales, sei whales, finback whales, killer whales, seals, penguins, and albatrosses. On the way, *Calypso* called at ports in Argentina, Patagonia, the Falkland Islands, and Terra del Fuego. Before leaving, she received a load of special equipment, including a Hughes 3000 helicopter, which can be disassembled and stored below deck; a helicopter landing pad on her stem; a hot-air balloon; special equipment for diving in antarctic waters; new cameras; new lighting equipment, and so forth.

Diving Saucers

There are several types of diving saucers, or minisubs, designed by Captain Cousteau and developed by the Center of Advanced Marine Studies of Marseilles:

— The SP-350, a two-passenger vehicle, is equipped with a cinematographic camera, a still camera, a hydraulically operated pincer and lift, and a storage basket. It has been used in more than 700 dives and is stored in *Calypso*'s aft hold.

— The SP-1000, or sea flea, carries only one man but was designed to be used in conjunction with a second SP-1000. It has two exterior cameras (16mm and 35mm), both controlled from the interior of the saucer, and tape recorders for recording underwater sounds. It has been used in more than 100 dives. Two SP-1000s can be stored aboard *Calypso*.

— The SP-4000, or Deepstar, is capable of diving to 4,000 feet. It was built for Westinghouse and was launched in 1966. It has participated in more than 500 dives. It is a two-passenger vehicle, with a speed of three knots.

— The SP-3000 was built for CNEX0. It travels at a speed of three knots and accommodates three passengers.

Appendix Two

The Pinnipeds (Pinnipedia)

The Pinnipeds are amphibious, carnivorous mammals which originally lived on dry land and then adapted to aquatic life. Their forepaws and hind paws were modified into swimming paddles by means of a membrane between the digits of the paws. They have short tails and are more numerous in the cold waters of the globe than in the warm areas.

The order of Pinnipedia contains three families:

Otaridae: sea lions, furred seals;

Odobenidae: walrus;

Phocidae: seals and elephant seals.

The smallest of the Pinnipeds is the *Phoca lispida* which is slightly over five feet in length and attains a weight of about 200 pounds. The largest is the elephant seal of the Antarctic, *Mirounga leonina,* some specimens of which reach a length of twenty-three feet and a weight of three and a half tons.

The Otaridae (Eared Seals)

Otaridae are carnivorous animals and live in groups. The males assemble harems of from fifteen to forty females, though sometimes the number of "wives" reaches eighty.

They have external ears and scrotum.

There are six varieties in the Pacific, along the Atlantic coast of South America, and along the Australian shore.

The *Otaridae* include the sea lions, whose downless coats are without commercial value. They are found along the Pacific coast of the American continent. *Neophoca* frequents the southern shore of Australia. The "trained seal" usually seen in circuses is the *Zalophus californianus* or California Sea Lion.

The Fur Seals retain their down, and their coats have considerable commercial value as pelts. The *Callorhinus,* or Nofthern Fur Seal, found in the Bering Sea, the Pribilof Islands, Alaska, and the Kuriles, has been hunted for its fur. *Arctocephalus* lives in antarctic waters, along the coasts of South America and Australia, in the Kerguelen Islands, etc.

The Odobenidae (Walruses)

Among the *Odobenidae,* or walruses, the upper canines grow into tusks which may reach a length of twenty-four inches. There is a single genus: *Odobenus,* and two subspecies: *Odobenus rosmarus rosmarus,* which is found in the North Atlantic, and *Odobenus rosmarus divergens,* which lives in the North Pacific.

Female walruses bear their young every two years. Gestation continues for at least one year. The largest specimens reach a length of about thirteen feet and weigh over a ton.

Only the *Otaridae* and the walruses have sufficiently sturdy forepaws and hind paws to move on land by raising their bodies. The other pinnipeds pull themselves along on their forepaws, with their stomachs and hindquarters dragging on the ground.

The Phocidae (Seals and Elephant Seals)

The hind paws of the *Phocidae,* unlike those of the *Otaridae,* do not fold under their bodies, and they have no external ears and scrotum. Some members of this family are monogamous and mate in the water. Others gather on land or on the ice in order to reproduce, and they mate successively with any available female.

There are four subfamilies of *Phocidae:*
— The *Phocinae,* represented by the genus *Phoca,* the most common of which

From top to bottom: a seal, a sea lion, a walrus, an elephant seal.

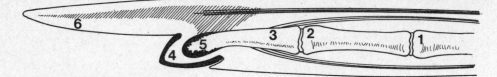

Finger of a pinniped (longitudinal view):

1. First phalanx
2. Second phalanx
3. Third phalanx
4. Nail, or claw
5. Fibro-cartilaginous covering of third phalanx.
6. Fibro-cartilaginous axis.

is the *Phoca vitulina,* or Harbor Seal, found along the western and northeastern coasts of the United States, off Baja California, and in northern European as well as Canadian waters.

— The *Lobodontinae,* which includes several genera:

　　Leptonychotes, or Weddell seal, which lives along the coast of Patagonia;

　　Lobodon carcinophagus, the crab-eating seal of the South Seas;

　　Hydrurga leptonyx, or sea leopard, also found in southern waters. It is a redoubtable beast of prey, feeding on penguins and young seals.

— The *Monachinae,* represented by *Monachus monachus,* the hooded, or monk seal of the Mediterranean, which also frequents the coastal waters of West Africa.

— The *Cystophorinae,* to which belongs the elephant seal (genus *Mirounga*). The elephant seal has its colonies and harems, not only on the island of Guadalupe but also on several islands in the South Seas (St. Paul, Kerguelen, etc.) where *Mirounga leonina* is found. The Guadalupe colony is another species, *Mirounga angustirostris,* which is also found off the coasts of California and Mexico, where it is on the road to extinction. This species is sedentary, unlike the members of the other species which scatter after mating and molting and about whose lives in the sea we know very little.

Right, above: Skeleton of a seal.
Right, below: Skeleton of a sea lion.
The differing forms of the pelvis are explained by the respective means of land-locomotion. Sea lions (and walruses) move on land by putting their weight on their hind members, while seals use their forepaws to drag their bodies along the ground. Thus, our sea lions, Pepito and Christobald, were able to "sit" while they were aboard *Calypso*.

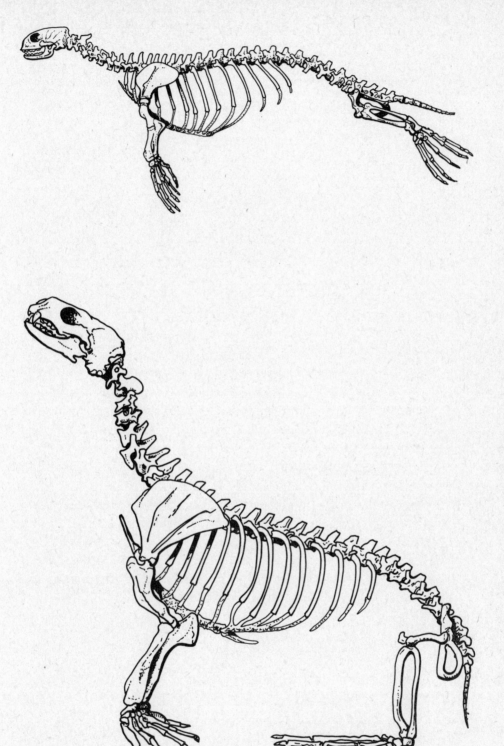

Appendix Three

The Eskimos

Eskimos are of Mongoloid appearance, though they are distinguished from true Mongols by their long, high skulls. They are a short, heavy-set people, with black hair and narrow eyes, and live in the arctic regions of North America, northeastern Asia, and Greenland. The Eskimo people today are divided among the governments of four countries: Denmark, Canada, the United States, and the U.S.S.R. They number only about 70,000, of which 23,000 are in Greenland, 9,500 in northern Canada, 25,000 in Alaska, and 1,300 in the north of Asia.

The origins of the Eskimo remain shrouded in mystery. A century ago, teams of Danish, American, and Russian archaeologists began a series of digs in areas where the ground, even in summer, remains half-frozen. A Dane, H. Larsen, discovered the most important site at Epioutak, Alaska, which included the remains of between 600 and 700 houses and 550 tombs. Larsen considered Canada to be "the cradle of Eskimo archaeology."

To H. B. Collins, "it is probably somewhere to the North and East of Lake Baikal that lie the undiscovered remains of the immediate ancestors of the Eskimo."

As we have noted in the text of the present work, a Soviet anthropologist,

Rudenko, places the origin of the Eskimo in Melanesia. It seems certain, in any event, that the Eskimo's high degree of culture, his technique for cutting stone, and his skill in making tools were brought by his ancestors from their original homeland.

R. Gessain has noted that "the oldest levels are those which show the highest degree of evolution, the greatest artistic development, and the greatest complexity."*

No one has offered a completely satisfactory explanation of the fact that, some six or eight thousand years B.C., a group of men chose to emigrate to one of the most hostile environments on the face of the earth. It has been suggested that they emigrated in order to escape invasions from other races, or in search of more plentiful game. Some historians believe that this migration northward was a consequence of the last ice age. According to this hypothesis, game animals — the caribou, the musk ox, the reindeer — were driven southward by the advancing glacier. Then, as the glacier retreated, the animals began moving northward in its wake, and prehistoric human hunters perhaps followed them.

This may be. The Eskimos are, in any case, the last prehistoric hunters on earth. They are men from the Stone Age, using spearheads of bone and stone arrowheads. Sculptures and engravings of ivory, found in abundance in the Arctic, and still in use today, bear witness to this prehistoric connection.

Most of the Eskimos of Greenland are of mixed blood. Many of them are part Danish. They do not call themselves Eskimos, but Greenlanders, or *Kaladlit*. Denmark, since its acquisition of Greenland in 1821, has been a diligent protector and promoter of the Eskimos, and demographic growth has been continuous.

The Eskimos, from their earliest history, have been a race of hunters, as distinguished from the Lapps, who are herders of reindeer.

The Eskimos, remote as they are from what is generally regarded as "civilization," have nonetheless reaped the least desirable consequences of human technology. In 1962, a scientific expedition visited the Arctic in order to study the effects of nuclear radiation caused by atomic explosions. It was found that the milk of Eskimo women, as well as that of bears and seals, contained from fifty to a hundred times more cesium-137 than that of Canadian mothers. Another study, conducted in 1972, has determined that the dosage of strontium-90 and cesium-137 had become, in ten years, somewhat less than the maximum dosage regarded as "safe." On the other hand, it was discovered that the amount of pesticides contained in the milk (and par-

* *Les Esquimaux du Groënland à l'Alaska.*

ticularly of DDT) was 60 per cent higher than the tolerable maximum, in both human milk and seal milk. Pollution of this sort, concentrated as it is in the fishes, in the marine mammals, and in the bears of the Arctic, is one of the greatest dangers facing the Far North.

Another problem is presented by the substitution of modern education for traditional Eskimo culture. The establishment of schools has served to separate children from their parents and has contributed to the creation of a "generation gap." The teaching of English in the schools has led Eskimo children to regard their own language with contempt; and the substitution of new techniques for the traditional skills has given rise to opposition between the young and the old.

There are even places in the Arctic where the new generation refuses to speak of the past of the Eskimo people and categorically rejects Eskimo culture. Yet, most often, these same young people are unable to integrate themselves into the Anglo-Saxon world.

More than the Americans or the Canadians, the Danes, in Greenland, have made some progress in preserving Eskimo traditions while providing Eskimo children with modern schools. The final solution will probably be found only when the teachers in those schools will themselves be of Eskimo origin. Such teachers will be in a position to preserve what is best in the culture of the Eskimos, including the Eskimo language which, although it has no written literature, is blessed with a striking richness of expression.

Appendix Four

Alaska

The central region of Alaska is mountainous and includes Mount McKinley, the highest peak in North America, as well as a large number of volcanoes. To the north, there are low, flat plains. The western coastline is very jagged and bordered by numerous islands.

One-quarter of Alaska's land lies within the Arctic Circle. The remainder is in the North Temperate Zone. Because of its vast extent and geographic situation and because the climate of the southern coast is tempered by warm ocean currents, temperature varies greatly from region to region. In southeast Alaska, for instance, there is not a great difference between winter and summer temperatures, and along the seacoast the average annual temperature is uniformly mild. However, in this area the rainfall is heavy. It is less so in the interior.

Typically arctic climate is found only in the northern and western parts of Alaska, to the Pribilof Islands and St. Lawrence Island. The summer lasts three months, and the climate is warm — not unlike that of the temperate regions. Winter, however, begins in September and lasts until May. There are very low temperatures and a great deal of snow, and the ground freezes solid. Because of the fog, the coastal tundra is quite damp and covered with permafrost. The frost melts slightly during the summer, and then moss, lichen, grass, and dwarf trees grow.

The Gold Rush

Alaska and the Aleutian Islands were first colonized by Russian huntsmen and trappers. These were followed by American seal hunters, and whalers infested the Bering Sea. Alaska was purchased from Russia by the United States in 1867, and gradually its wealth in natural resources — furs, wood, fish — came to light.

In 1897, gold was found in the Yukon, and the area was flooded with prospectors. It was the great gold rush of '97, immortalized by Jack London, who had a part in it, and memorialized later by Charlie Chaplin. In a single year, 100,000 persons landed at Skagway, Alaska, to begin the seven-hundred-mile trek to Dawson City, in the Klondike, and, they hoped, to wealth. First, however, they had to cross the terrible Chilkoot saddle, and each man was required by the Canadian Mounted Police to carry one ton of supplies with him, in individual loads of one hundred pounds.

Alaska was no less rich in gold than the Yukon. Juneau, Nome, and Fairbanks — the "heart of gold" of Alaska — had gold rushes of their own. Even today, Alaska produces some 14,000 pounds of gold annually, as opposed to Canada's 24,000 pounds.

Alaska's population today is 300,000 — double what it was in 1950.

One man out of every three in Alaska is a member of the armed forces of the United States, for the state is of great strategic importance. Alaska and the U.S.S.R. are separated, at certain points, only by a few miles of water. In 1950, the United States and Canada undertook the establishment of a radar chain stretching across the Arctic: the "Ballistic Missile Early Warning System," which was intended to detect Russian rockets. American and Russian planes make daily flights over the North Pole, and both nations now maintain military stations on floating islands of ice in the Arctic, which are supplied by air.

Oil and Uranium

The enormous wealth of Alaska consists of oil and natural gas (south of Point Barrow), coal and minerals (gold, silver, mercury, antimony, tin, copper, iron, uranium, platinum, and lead). Its chief industries, however, are fishing and canning. The salmon industry, which makes use of the most advanced equipment, does an annual business of between $40 and $50 million.

Animals are abundant, and fur (fox, wolf, lynx, seal, etc.) ranks third among Alaska's industries, after fishing and mining.

A projected dam on the Yukon River, at Rampart Canyon, will soon provide some 5,000 kw. of electrical power to the state. The U. S. Army has already built two nuclear reactors of 1,500 kw. each, one in Alaska and the other in Greenland.

The departure of André's balloon, on July 11, 1897, for the North Pole. André and his two companions were never heard from again.

Appendix Five

The Discovery of the Arctic

The first arctic explorer whose name is known to history was Phtheas, a mariner of Marseilles, who, some three centuries before the birth of Christ, reached a land which he named Ultima Thule. It is believed today that Ultima Thule was the modern city of Trondhjem, on the Norwegian coast.

It was only some twelve centuries later, in the ninth century A.D., that the Vikings discovered Iceland and that the famed Erik the Red established colonies on Greenland which were to last for over five hundred years. But the Vikings did not stop there. In their sturdy *drakkars,* they explored the coasts of Newfoundland and Labrador. There is no record of the information they derived from these explorations; and the Viking settlements on Greenland disappeared in the fourteenth century, leaving no evidence as to the reason for their abandonment.

In the sixteenth century, the first systematic explorations of the Arctic were undertaken. Elizabeth I of England dispatched one of her most experienced captains, Sir Martin Frobisher, to find a passage between the West and the East — the famous Northwest Passage which was to haunt the imagination of explorers for the next three hundred years.

A Dutch navigator, William Barentz, made three voyages into the Arctic in search of a northeast passage. He discovered the Spitzberg, but his ship, the *Discovery,* was trapped in the ice and he was forced to winter beyond the Arctic Circle. This was the first instance of man surviving a winter in the polar regions. Barentz is considered the first of the great heroes of polar exploration.

Henry Hudson, with the backing of English merchants, sailed up the coast of Greenland to 80° 23′, and thus established a record which was to stand for the next 166 years. In 1609, during another voyage, he discovered the bay which bears his name and thought that he had discovered the long-sought passage between the Atlantic and the Pacific.

A Danish navigator, Vitus Jonassen Bering, entered the service of Peter the Great and devoted thirty-six years of his life to the exploration of the Arctic. In 1741, he entered the strait which today is known as the Bering Strait and claimed Alaska on behalf of Russia.

During the whole of the eighteenth century, many mariners persisted in the arctic search for an open passage from East to West or from West to East. To encourage such undertakings, the British Government offered a prize of 20,000 pounds to the navigator who discovered the Northwest Passage. In 1845, the same government organized the most elaborate polar expedition the world had ever seen. For the first time, two steam-and-propeller ships, the *Erebus* and the *Terror,* entered arctic water. The commander of the expedition was Sir John Franklin, whose mission was specifically to discover the Northwest Passage. The expedition sailed with 168 men and enough supplies for a four-year voyage. For three years, nothing was heard from Sir John or his ships. Finally, Lady Franklin succeeded in stirring public opinion to the extent that ships were dispatched to discover the fate of the expedition. The rescue ships found thirty bodies of Sir John's men and nothing more. The fate of the expedition has remained a mystery to this day.

The Northwest Passage and the Northeast Passage were both sought with diligence during the last half of the nineteenth century. Commander McClure set an example for determination when he took four years to make his way from the Pacific to the Atlantic, using two ships — the *Investigator* and the *Resolute* — then making part of the journey on foot before boarding the *Polar Star* for the last leg of the journey. In 1879, Eric Adolph Nordenskjold, a Swede, sailed along the northern coast of Asia and finally reached the Pacific Ocean through the Bering Strait. He had discovered the Northeast Passage, and the voyage had been made without loss of men and without the slightest damage to his ship, the *Vega.*

In the course of the preceding expeditions, no one had attempted to reach the North Pole. It was not until 1879 that an American naval officer,

Lieutenant George Washington De Long, organized an expedition for that purpose. The undertaking was financed by James Gordon Bennett, publisher of the New York *Herald;* the same James Gordon Bennett who had already sent Stanley to Africa in search of Dr. Livingstone. De Long's ship, however, was crushed against the ice, and he and his men took refuge on an ice floe where they remained for one hundred and forty agonizing days.

Another attempt to reach the Pole shared a similar fate when a small U. S. Army detachment, under the command of Captain Adolphus W. Greely, landed at Discovery Harbor, on Ellesmere Island. The detachment, when its supplies failed to arrive as planned, began moving southward. It reached Bedford Pym Island, where a rescue team met them. Of Captain Greely's twenty-nine men, only seven were still alive. They had survived by eating algae, lichen, flies, their belts, and even their sleeping bags.

In 1893, a Norwegian, Fridtjof Nansen, conceived the audacious plan of allowing himself to drift aboard a ship imprisoned in the ice, in the hope that he would be carried to the North Pole, or at least to a very high latitude. His ship, the *Fram,* was designed and constructed to withstand the enormous pressure exerted by the ice. Nansen remained aboard the *Fram* for two years, in the midst of the ice. Finally, he concluded that the ship would never reach the Pole, and he and several companions left the *Fram* and continued northward by dog sled until they came within 250 miles of the Pole. There, however, they were forced to turn back for lack of supplies.

The man who was to conquer the North Pole was an American engineer, Robert E. Peary. Peary had spent some twenty years in the Arctic before attempting the feat which was to bring him fame, and he put that experience to good use in planning his expedition. Unlike his predecessors, he was determined to reach the Pole during the winter — a season which earlier explorers had dreaded and avoided. His reasoning was that, during the winter, the ice and snow would level the terrain and fill the canyons and crevasses, and thereby make his passage less arduous. He also planned to travel with a minimum of equipment, using dogs and sleds and wearing Eskimo clothing. And, finally, Peary was sustained by a deep conviction that he was the man appointed by destiny to reach the Pole.

Despite Peary's careful planning and his unshakable determination, his early attempts were not altogether successful. Three times, he started out for the Pole. In March 1902, with one sled, ten dogs, three Eskimos, and his black servant, Henson, he reached 84° 17′ — and was forced to turn back. In 1905, he tried again with a new ship, the *Roosevelt,* and reached 87° 6′. Then, having eaten his dogs for food and burned his sled for warmth, he was compelled to return.

In 1908, Robert Peary once more set sail aboard the *Roosevelt*. With his Eskimo friends and Henson, he debarked at Cape Columbia. Before him lay more than four hundred miles of ice. He started out on February 22, 1909, with a party of twenty-four men, fifteen sleds, and 133 dogs. The expedition was divided into six groups, with the advance guard consisting of Peary himself, Matt Henson — who was a skilled sled driver — and four Eskimos. When a point only seventy-five miles from the Pole was reached, Peary's team set out alone with five sleds and ten dogs. For five days they moved across the ice and snow — five days in which Peary suffered terribly from his frozen feet. On the fifth day, the team reached 89° 57'. "The Pole was in sight," Peary wrote, "but I lacked the strength to make the last few steps. The accumulated fatigue of all those days and all those nights, the sleepless marches, all fell upon me at once. I was too exhausted even to understand that the dream of my life had been realized."

On April 6, 1909, at 10 A.M., Robert Peary planted the American flag at the North Pole. Then he built an igloo for himself and remained within it for two days without sleeping. After twenty-three years of work and planning, and several failures, he had attained his goal.

Peary had been unwilling to allow any other white man to share his glory with him. His sole companions, and the only witnesses to his accomplishment, were four Eskimos and a black servant. He was to pay for his lack of foresight, for the testimony of his witnesses was soon challenged. Another American, Dr. Frederick Cook, a former companion of Peary's, claimed to have reached the Pole on April 21, 1908 — almost a year before Peary himself. A violent and public polemic ensued to which not even the death of the two principals put an end. Today, it is impossible to say, with absolute certainty, which of the two men was actually the first to reach the Pole.

Man first traveled through the Arctic by ship, then on foot and with dog sleds, and finally by air. A Swedish flier, Andrée, attempted to fly over the Pole in a balloon in 1897. For years, nothing was heard of Andrée. Then, a polar expedition found his body, and that of his companions, half-eaten by bears.

It was not until 1926 that man succeeded in flying over the Pole. The hero, in this case, was an American, Admiral William Byrd, flying alone in his aircraft, the *Josephine Ford*. Only two days later, however, on May 11, 1926, the dirigible *Norge*, commanded by Captain Nobile, an Italian, also passed over the North Pole.

Another aerial expedition under Captain Nobile's command, in 1928, ended unhappily when the dirigible was forced to land on an ice floe. There was a great outburst of public indignation when it was learned that Nobile had been the first man to be evacuated by a Swedish rescue aircraft, while the five other survivors were compelled to wait for a month on the ice floe until a Russian icebreaker, the *Krassine,* came to their rescue.

Finally, on May 21, 1937, a four-engine Soviet airplane, the *Ant-6,* landed at the North Pole, and four scientists debarked. They were to remain there for nine months, allowing themselves to be carried by the current to Greenland. For the first time, the North Pole was inhabited.

The terror which the polar regions inspired in man not more than a half-century ago now seems remote indeed. Today, commercial airliners fly daily over the frozen wastes on the polar route between Europe and Asia. One more unknown region of the globe has been opened to satisfy man's curiosity.

It remains to be seen how man will make use of this opportunity. History shows that when confronted by a new land, our first impulse is to destroy what we find there in order to create a new land in an image familiar to us — as we are currently engaged in doing in what was once "darkest Africa". We can only hope that the heightened consciousness of the public with respect to ecological and environmental values will enable the Arctic to fare better at our hands.

ILLUSTRATED GLOSSARY

Apnoea

The suspension, of more or less long duration, of breathing.

Aponevrose

The fibrous membrane which envelops a muscle and resists its lateral movement when there is a contraction.

Ascension Island

An island of the Atlantic, situated about seven hundred miles northwest of St. Helena to which it is administratively attached. It has an area of about fifty square miles and five hundred inhabitants.

The island was discovered by Juan de Nova, a Portuguese navigator, on the Feast of the Ascension in 1501 and became a British possession in 1815.

Ascidians, or Sea Squirts

Ascidians are chordates and tunicates. The ascidian, also known as the sea squirt, is in effect a small water bag, yellow or red, which is free-floating as a larva but becomes fixed at the adult stage. There are two openings: one to take in the sea water from which the ascidian takes oxygen and the tiny organisms on which it feeds and the other to "squirt" out the waste water.

Despite their primitive appearance, ascidians have gills, a stomach, an intestine, and a V-shaped heart which drives blood through the animal's body sometimes in one direction and sometimes in the other: eighty pulsations in one direction, then forty in the other. They are hermaphroditic, having both a testicle and an ovary.

The so-called "violets," regarded as a delicacy along the Riviera, are ascidians.

Azoic

An adjective describing an area which contains no living creature.

Bering, Vitus

Vitus Bering (or Behring) was a Danish seaman and explorer who lived from 1681 to 1741. He was in the employ of Russia, and he explored Kamchatka, discovered Alaska, the Aleutian Islands, and Kodiak Island.

Bering Straits, named in his honor, is the passageway between the Pacific and the Arctic oceans.

Blackfish, or Pilot Whale

The pilot whale, or blackfish, has a rounded head, the upper part of which projects over the upper jaw. It attains a length of between fourteen and twenty-five feet and, as its name indicates, is wholly black. It has a dorsal fin and between seven and eleven teeth in each jaw.

The blackfish feeds mainly on squid. During the summer, it is found near the Newfoundland coast. It winters in warm waters, where the young are born. Gestation lasts twelve months. The mating season is in the autumn. Males mature sexually at three years, and females at six.

Blackfish are the chief whale resource of Newfoundland, and between three and four thousand of these small whales are killed there every year.

Closed-Circuit Oxygen Breathing Apparatus

An underwater breathing device, similar to that used by British frogmen during World War II, which removed carbon dioxide from the diver's air by means of a filter cartridge. It is silent, since it does not release air bubbles in the water. It is frequently used by *Calypso*'s divers to approach marine animals without frightening them.

Conshelf III

Conshelf III is the name given to an experiment undertaken off Cape Ferrat in 1965. Six divers lived for three weeks in an "underwater house," some three hundred feet below the surface. The predecessor of this experiment was Conshelf II, which took place in 1963, in the Red Sea. During the latter experiment, two men lived at a depth of eighty feet for a week, and a team of eleven men remained at a depth of thirty-five feet for a month.

Cormorant

The cormorant is a marine bird of the Steganopod order. The two varieties, the great cormorant and the green cormorant, are both found as far north as the edge of the Arctic Circle.

The great cormorant is black and is very widespread. The breeding grounds are at Greenland, Iceland, and Labrador. It dives mostly in coastal waters and rarely in the open sea.

The green cormorant is smaller than the great cormorant and dives less deeply. In order to reduce its buoyancy, it dampens its feathers before diving.

Ecology

The science which studies the environment in which beings live and reproduce and the relationship of those beings to the environment.

Electrocardiograph

An apparatus which records the functioning of the heart by the graphic transcription of the electrical phenomena which occur during that functioning.

Europa

A small island three hundred miles west of Africa, Europa is only six miles in diameter, including a brackish shallow lagoon and huge beaches of golden sand. It is a favorite mating and egg-laying place for sea turtles.

Europa is a storm-warning station, and four men are stationed there permanently. These meteorologists are citizens of Réunion, for though the island is French, it is attached administratively to the *département* of Réunion.

Floe

An ice floe is a detached slab of floating ice. When several floes annex, they form a "pack."

Gannet, or Booby

The gannet is a large marine bird of the order of Steganopods. It lives in colonies of several hundred individuals. It feeds by diving and attacking fish from their underside. Usually, it swallows the fish underwater.

Gull

The gull is a coastal and oceanic bird of the order of Charadriiforms. It is quite common in subarctic and arctic regions. Although the gull usually feeds on dead fishes and coastal plankton, it also eats whatever it finds on land and in lakes and swamps.

Hawser

A thick line used to secure a ship. Hawsers are made of manilla, hemp, steel, or nylon.

Huskies

Huskies, or sled dogs, vary by breed, size, and characterisitics according to the region in which they are found. The Malemute, used in northwestern Canada, resembles the wolf from which it is descended. The true husky, or Eskimo dog, is a crossbreed of wolf and various Asiatic dogs and is much heavier than the Malemute. The Samoyed is the Siberian sled dog.

All of these breeds are extremely hardy and have thick coats which protect them from the cold. They were long man's indispensable helpers in the Arctic, but they have been gradually replaced by motor vehicles.

An eskimo with his dogs and his sled can move over the snow at a speed of eighteen miles per hour, and for eighteen hours at a stretch.

Ice Cap

The "ice caps" are the permanent covering of ice found at both the North and South poles. The amount of melting is insignificant because of the everlasting cold.

Kelp

Kelp is the common name given, particularly in the United States, to various large algae, most of them pheophytes, which are found off the coast of California and Mexico. They are also found near New Zealand, Argentina, Chile, and Peru.

Macrocystis pyrifera reaches a length of nearly two hundred feet. Its base is firmly anchored in the bottom, and its strands float by virtue of air-filled bladders. It grows very rapidly. Some authorities believe that this species grows to a length of one thousand or fifteen hundred feet.

Along with several other algae, *Macrocystis pyrifera, Pelagophycus porra,* and *Eisenia arbores* are known generically as kelp.

Kerguelen Islands

A subantarctic archipelago in the southern Indian Ocean. The temperature is oceanic, and though it remains above freezing and varies only five degrees between summer and winter, the weather is consistently foul.

There is little vegetation, and the islands, a French possession, have limited economic interest.

Killer Whale, or Orc

The killer whale is a member of the Delphinidae family of the Odontoceti, or toothed cetaceans, genus *Orcinus*. It travels in schools and attains a length of about twenty feet and a weight of one ton. It is black, with white markings on its underside extending from the lower jaw to the middle of the stomach. There is another, smaller white spot above the eyes. The jaws each contain between twenty and twenty-eight teeth.

Killer whales prefer warm-blooded prey: seals, dolphins, and walruses. They mate between November and January, and gestation lasts from eleven to twelve months. The mother nurses her calf for a year following birth.

Kodiak Bear

The Kodiak, or brown bear, *Ursus arctos middendorffi,* when standing erect, is sometimes over eight feet tall. It may attain a weight of fifteen hundred pounds.

The Kodiak bear is the largest land carnivore presently in existence. It feeds chiefly on fish and especially on salmon which it catches in abundance when these fish are moving upstream on their migrations. Yet the bear has very poor eyesight, and it fishes almost blindly.

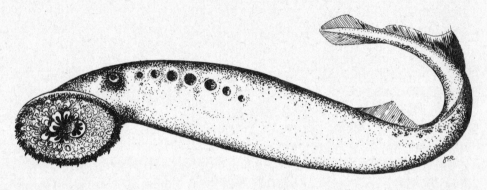

The lamprey is a migratory carnivore. Its mouth, which acts as a sucker disk, is equipped with sharp teeth which enable the lamprey both to attach itself to a victim and to cut into the victim's flesh. The lamprey's denticulated tongue then digs into the flesh.

Lamprey

An elongated fish with a cylindrical body and a circular mouth.

The lamprey was formerly classified as a fish; now it is regarded as a vertebrate and classified among the Agnathae — which are characterized by the absence of a lower jaw. The lamprey's tooth-lined mouth acts as a suction cup and allows the animal to lead a semiparasitic life by attaching itself to the bodies of fishes or cetaceans. It has seven branchial orifices, circular in form, which give it the appearance of a flute.

Longwood

The house on St. Helena designated as Napoleon's residence after his final exile in 1815. The fallen emperor died there.

The building was erected originally as a storehouse for the East India Company. Later, it was converted into a country house for the deputy governor of the island. It has twenty rooms. For nine months of the year, Longwood is a prey to unbearable humidity. For the remaining three months, it is exposed to constant wind.

Lupine

A herbaceous plant of the Papillonacae family. Some species are cultivated as ornamentals.

Maldive Islands

An archipelago situated in the Indian Ocean, at the southern tip of India, the Maldives were once a port of call for sailing vessels and an important stopover along the historic Spice Route. Today, they are only a string of poor, rarely visited coral islands.

The Maldives were colonized by the Portuguese but became a British possession early in the nineteenth century. They gained full independence in 1965.

Among male narwhals, one of the teeth on the left side of the upper jaw attains a considerable size. During the Middle Ages, this tooth, or tusk, was prized as the fabled "unicorn's horn" of legend.

Narwhal

The narwhal is a toothed cetacean of the family *Monodontidae*. It inhabits the arctic seas, keeping to coastal waters and occasionally venturing into the mouths of rivers.

Its length varies from ten to sixteen or seventeen feet — not counting its spirally twisted tusk, slightly to the right of the snout, which may grow to a length of nine feet. The tusk — actually a tooth — is found only in the male.

The narwhal has no dorsal fin but only a slight protrusion, or "crest."

Contrary to what is commonly believed, the narwhal's tusk is not used to break ice, nor as a weapon. It seems likely, in fact, that it has no use at all.

In other times, the tusk was thought to be the "horn" of the fabled unicorn and was very highly regarded for the medical powers attributed to it. The purveyors of these "unicorn horns" were Norwegian fishermen who hunted the narwhal in Iceland and Greenland.

The narwhal travels in groups of six to ten individuals, with the females often traveling separately from the males. They eat cuttlefish, crustaceans, and fish.

The period of gestation is unknown. The calf, at birth, measures four and one-half feet in length and remains with the mother for a time.

Pedicel

The pedicel is a complex organ found in the bodies of certain echinoderms, especially starfishes and sea urchins. It comprises a tiny claw armed with two or three jaws, at the ends of which there is a pointed tooth or fang. The latter sometimes is connected to a gland containing a venom.

The pincer is activated by muscles and by a ganglion covered with sensitive cells. It is a formidable weapon. If an enemy or a prey comes within reach, it is seized by the claw, pierced by the jaws, and then paralyzed by the venom.

Penguin

Antarctic penguins belong to the order Impennes and to the Spheniscidae family. They are perfectly adapted to marine life. Their feather-covered wings are used for swimming.

The penguin is able to survive in extremely low temperatures and to go without food for long periods. It feeds on fish, crustaceans, worms, and mollusks, and is found in antarctic and subantarctic regions. It is also found in the Galápagos Islands because of the presence there of the cold waters of the Humboldt Current.

Planking

The exterior covering of a ship or boat.

Proboscidians

The term proboscidians is derived from the Greek word *proboskis,* meaning trunk, and it designates a suborder of ungulate mammals, of large size, possessing a prehensile trunk.

The first proboscidians appeared in Africa some fifty million years ago, the descendants of a small mammal which lived during the Paleocene or Eocene periods. One variety of proboscidian, the mastodon, was found practically everywhere on the globe. The trilophodons reached North America at the end of the Miocene period. The Amebelodon, whose remains have been found in Nebraska, had shovel-shaped tusks.

The race eventually evolved into the *Mastodon americanus,* which had a thick coat of fur, and into the mammoth.

The sole surviving proboscidians are the African and Indian elephants.

Puffin

The puffin belongs to the order of Charadriiforms. It is a bird of the Arctic Sea and of the cold temperate zones of the Northern Hemisphere. It feeds on fish and small marine fauna which it catches by diving. The puffin lives in colonies, which are sometimes quite large, on the faces of cliffs or in burrows.

St. Helena

A volcanic island, belonging to Great Britain, situated about eleven hundred miles west of Africa. It has an area of seventy-five square miles and a population of forty-six hundred. The capital is Jamestown.

St. Helena was discovered by the Portuguese in 1502 and annexed by the Dutch, who conveyed it to England in 1659.

It was the place of exile of Napoleon in 1815 and of his death in 1821.

Sea Otter

The sea otter (*Enhydra lutris*) is a mammal of the Mustelidae family. It lives along the Pacific coast of the northern United States and feeds chiefly on mollusks.

It may reach a length of over six feet, and it is well adapted to marine life.

Its coat is quite valuable, and the species is threatened with extinction because they have been hunted so widely for their fur.

A *Solaster papposus* — a starfish whose arms exceed by far the usual five of the ordinary starfish.

Solaster

The solaster, or sun star, is an echinoderm. It belongs to the class Asteroidea, order of Phanerozonia, genus *Solaster*.

The sun star lives in cold waters along both shores of the Atlantic. It is a voracious eater. Its colors are quite vivid, and it sometimes has as many as seventeen arms.

Sonar

Sonar is the acronym for Sound Navigation Ranging, an underwater detection and communication device analogous to radar and based upon the reflection of sonic and supersonic waves.

Starfish

Starfish, or sea stars, are echinoderms whose bodies are in the shape of a star with five branches or "arms." Some species have more than five branches. At the extremity of each arm, there is a short tentacle and at the base of that tentacle is a bright red, light-sensitive sensory organ. In addition, each arm has, on its underside, hundreds of tiny podia, or tube feet, equipped with suction disks. The starfish, therefore, is more mobile than its appearance would suggest.

It is a dedicated carnivore, devouring mollusks and crustaceans which have molted, both living and dead. Being unable to swallow its victim, the starfish everts its stomach and applies it to the victim, dissolving it in digestive juices.

In order to open the shells of bivalves such as oysters, the starfish will fold its arms over the oyster and pull until the oyster's shell begins to give way and a small opening appears. Then, the starfish's stomach is inserted into the opening and the oyster is digested.

The starfish is remarkable for its regenerative powers. If it loses one or more arms, or even part of the central disk that is its body, it can quickly grow new parts.

Suction Disk

An adhesive organ found among cephalopods, worms, and echinoderms which allows these animals to attach themselves to an object, to move, or to seize their prey. Among the cephalopods (octopuses, cuttlefish, etc.), the suction disks on the animal's arms have a circular corneous ring. A circular muscle, by contracting, reduces the diameter of the disk. A nerve in the arm leads to a ganglion in the peduncle, where the suction disk is located.

Tapir

The tapir is an ungulate animal (Tapiridae) whose nose ends in a short, prehensile trunk. It is not, however, a proboscidian, but a perissodactyl. The family includes four species, one of which is found in tropical Asia and the other three in Central America.

Territory

Territory is the space on land, or in the water or air, which an animal, or a group of animals, regards as its property. Many territorial species do not allow animals of other species to enter their territory. This is the case with the grouper, whose behavior was described in *Life and Death in a Coral Sea* and in *The Shark.*

It appears that an animal, in defending its territory, possesses a special strength and energy which almost always allows it to defeat the intruder.

Vaucluse Fountain

The Vaucluse Fountain is a well or pit located in France. It lies at the foot of a vertical cliff and is the source of a small river, the Sorgue. It is one of the great hydrological riddles of our time, and Captain Cousteau and his associates have made several dives there. It has not yet been possible to reach the bottom of the Fountain, or to find the means by which it communicates with a subterranean spur of the Sorgue. The water of the Fountain is extremely cold, and there is a whirlpool which makes diving very dangerous.

Bibliography

Birket-Smith, K., *Moeurs et Coutumes des Esquimaux*. Paris, 1937.

Braun, Patrick, *Les Hommes du Grand Nord*. Paris, 1973.

Gessain, R., *Les Esquimaux du Groenland à l'Alaska,* Paris, 1947.

Harrington, Richard, *Le Visage de l'Arctique*. Paris, 1957.

Jacobin, Lou, *Guide to Alaska and the Yukon*. Anchorage, 1963.

Ley, Willy, *The Poles*. New York, 1971.

Lockley, R. M., *Grey Seal, Common Seal*. London, 1966.

Malaurie, Jean, *Les Derniers Rois de Thule*. Paris, 1955.

Matthews, L. Harrison, *L'Éléphant de Mer*. Paris, 1953.

Poncins, G. de, *Kalbouna*. Paris, 1948.

Stonehouse, Bernard, *Les Animaux du Grand Nord*. Paris, 1972.

Vercel, Roger, *À l'Assaut des Poles*. Paris, 1938.

Victor, Paul-Emile, *Boréal*. Grasset, 1938.

— — —, *Banquise*. Paris, 1939.

Walker, Ernest P., *Mammals of the World*. Baltimore, 1968.

INDEX